LYRICAL LIVING

A Collection of Poetic Musings

James W. Tayburn

Lyrical Living – A collection of poetic musings
© 2017 by James W. Tayburn

All rights reserved, including the right to reproduce this work in any form without written permission from the publisher, except for brief passages in connection with non-commercial purposes. In all cases credit must be given to the original author.

For information or inquiries, visit www.dogoodbooks.com

ISBN: 978-0-9993095-0-6

Published by Do Good Books
First edition, August, 2017

Cover photo © Kent Banta. Used by permission.

For Friends and Family

Table of Contents

Introduction	xiii
Acknowledgments	xiv

1 Arizona — 1
Catalina Mountain Moods	3
Heaven On Earth	5
Land of Diversity	7
Standing Tall	9

2 Charities — 11
IMPACT Providing a Lifeline in Southern Arizona	13
Waiting To Smile	15

3 Commentary — 17
In Vino, Veritas	19
Stroke of the Pen	20
When Did The Rose Petals Fall To Earth?	22

4 Inspirational — 25
1st Corinthians Love	27
A Call to Action	28
A Poet's Rendition of the 23rd Psalm	29

A Poet's Alternate Rendition of the 23rd Psalm	30
Circle of Life	31
Enough	33
How Does Your Garden Grow?	35
I Woke Up This Morning and I'm Not Dead	36
In Full Bloom	38
In Full Bloom Revisited	40
It's The Heart	42
Pandora's Box	43
Simmer in Prayer	44
Steady Your Brother's Ladder	45
That Changed Everything	46
The Big Room	47
Thorns Always Come With The Rose	49
Today is a Gift	50
Traveling The Back Roads	52
Twelve Ordinary Men	54
Wildflower	56
You and I	58
Your Guardian Angel	60

5 Dogs — 63

D.O.G., Delight of God	64
Joy in the Now	65

6 Family and Friends — 67

A New Star in Heaven	69
A Standing Ovation	70
A Year Ago Today	71
Always in My Heart	73
Amazing Grace	74
Chandlers' Wedding Program	76
Diamonds Are Forever	77
Emma — One of a Kind	78
Fifty Golden Years	80
Forty Years and Counting	83
Friend	85
Gone	86
If the Lord Came to Call	87
Inner Voice	88
It is Finished: It is Beginning	90
Jake, the J-Man	91
Just a Friend	93
On the Way To Fifty	95
Our Little Girl	96
Our Spanish Daughter	98
Short Poems for Family	99
The Answered Prayer	101
Twenty and a Score	103

You Were There   104

7 Golf   107

But Then   109
Golf's Twilight Zone   110
Ode to Bogey   112
Pledge of Golf   116
The Game That Came Down From Heaven   117
The LINKS Player's Creed   119
The Shot   120

8 Holidays   123

America's Blessings   125
Christmas Highlights   126
Christmas Reflections   128
Christmas, the Acronym   131
No Room at the Inn   132
Reflect on Him   133
Thanksgiving Blessing   134
That Ordinary You   135
The Greatest Gift Exchange of All   137
The Ultimate Gift   138

9 On Getting Old — 141

A New Passion — 143
The Older I Get — 145

10 Travel — 147

Arctic Accolades — 149
He's Alive — 152
Icicle River — 154
Irish Memories — 155
Israel in a Minute — 157
Old Blue Eyes and Dr. No — 158
Remembering Bermuda — 159
Standing on the Galilee — 161

About the Author — 163

Introduction

    I don't know when I first started writing poetry, or why, but I suspect it had to do with a special occasion for a family member, business associate, or good friend. Since I retired I have had more time to write and many more poems have followed. My wife of fifty years, Marie, and many of my closest friends, have encouraged me for some time to have them published in a book. This is the result of that encouragement. If just one of them strikes a chord with you, this effort will have been worthwhile.
    A couple of final comments—while I have read some wonderful poems that do not incorporate rhyme, you won't see that in this collection because I'm very big on creating verses that rhyme. Lastly, while there are some "whimsical" selections included in this book, I try to author poems with a point or message, as I think you'll see. I hope you enjoy this collection.

JWT

Acknowledgments

A number of my great friends have encouraged me to publish a book of poems for some time, and I have resisted for quite a few years. There are a lot of people who, like me, write poetry for a hobby, and I never felt my poems were worthy of being published. But then, having been made aware of the importance of having this book as a legacy for my children and grandchildren, and finding a way to publish, I finally succumbed, and this book is the result.

At the risk of leaving someone out who is very important to me, I would like to thank these outstanding friends of mine for their encouragement: Dave and Joanne Thomas, Greg and Carol Tarr, Allen and Dorothy DeHart, Tex and Carole Whitney, and all of my friends at Bible Study and Links Players. Then there is Kent Banta who is an excellent photographer and artist who allowed me to use one of his outstanding Arizona landscape photographs for the cover of this book. I would also like to thank Lewis Greer who has been a huge help in getting this book published by knowing the ins and outs of how to get it done. Last, and most important, I would like to thank my wife, Marie, who kept encouraging me, pushing me, and initially organizing this collection of poems in a form that was amenable to being published. She has been an amazing lifelong partner in so many ways.

There are three poems I have to talk about specifically and give credit to the people who originally came up with the idea behind those poems. The first is Allen DeHart whose idea it was for the poem, *A Call to Action*, the second is Steve Wilson who originated the idea for the poem, *That Ordinary You*, and the third is Kent Banta who was the inspiration for the poem, *The Greatest Gift Exchange of All*. I'm thankful to all three of them, not only for their input on the poems, but more importantly for being great friends who have been big supporters of mine.

1
Arizona

We had lived in a number of places during my career, but until we retired, we had never lived west of the Mississippi. My first exposure to Arizona was for a national sales meeting in Phoenix and I immediately fell in love with the state—the warm weather year round, the wild animals, the unusual plants, and the mountains. These poems reflect that love.

Catalina Mountain Moods

I went to the mountains; only emptiness there
Hawks and their buddies had flown south somewhere
Animals along the ground had departed for water and food
And the mountain was engrossed in a somber mood

I went to the mountains; snow-covered its peaks
In the quiet of the moment, nature still speaks
Crisp, clean air permeates my waiting lungs
And my soul is hostage to the glistening sun

I went to the mountains, black as could be
Dark and foreboding robbed my security
Uneasiness settles over that sinister mount
As if some unseen calamity is about to play out

I went to the mountains; nothing could I see
A foggy mist sequesters its ridges in canopy
This ghastly shroud stokes my latent fears
And I'm comforted when it finally clears

I went to the mountains, ominous clouds on high
Lightning, God's laser show, arcs across the sky
Thunder jolts me from my stuporous trance
First raindrops strike the rocks and dance

I went to the mountains, feeling quite low
But my spirit was lifted by a double rainbow
No matter how troublesome or challenging the day
Rainbows are God's promise that all is OK

I went to the mountains, clothed emerald green
Watched plants spring to life and animals preen
Listened carefully and heard the refrain
Of nature's joyous acceptance of monsoon rain

I went to the mountains, golden in drape
Saguaros step out from the desert landscape
Rocks acquire a luster with the evening light
Afternoon's radiant showcase gives way to the night

I went to the mountains, Beethoven there
Hawks and turkey vultures float on a carpet of air
It's nature's symphony played out before our eyes
As they dip below the horizon, then catch a thermal and rise

I went to the mountains, clouds all apuff
Fill my senses with their winsome fluff
They hang there on the cliffs, attached it seems
It's a magical time and it fuels my dreams

I went to the mountains in the darkness of night
A silhouette against the sky, reflecting power and might
A billion stars captivate the setting as only they can
A full moon perches on the ridge, as if placed there by hand

I go to the mountains, sometimes only in mind
As I extend my gaze upward, here's what I find
Each interlude is different, always mesmerizing and new,
And I say "thank you Lord for this magnificent view."

Heaven On Earth

Dear God, thank you for bringing us to this place
Your awesome creation to savor and taste
We know Earth cannot match Heaven's look
But we must be close, here at SaddleBrooke

Lord, we gaze at the mountain vistas and valleys green
Behold the desert bloom and starscape serene
It fills our being and restores our soul
Our faith replenished; our self made whole

There really is a place, this Arizona home
Where deer and antelope still do roam
Where coyote, wildcat, and jackrabbit play
And skies really are not cloudy all day

There's a heavenly solitude to these grounds
It permeates our spirit as we meander around
Only on occasion does serenity lack
As a golf ball is given a mighty whack

The games we play interrupt the quail
Roadrunners dart across our trail
Black cardinals induce us to pause and muse
And mourning doves awaken us with their coos

We who live here are affected, in turn
Life can be simpler we finally learn
Here, in this place, where everyone's equal
All of us previously important people

We breathe deeply, inhaling the beauty surround
We pause, we listen, we hear not a sound
The rat race seemingly eons away
Much like the Garden in Adam's day

Dear God, thank you for bringing us to this place
Your awesome creation to savor and taste
We know Earth cannot match Heaven's look
But we must be close, here at SaddleBrooke.

Land of Diversity

We've heard it said there are no seasons in this desert land
All the days monotonously boring and landscape bland
Winter, Spring, Summer, Fall all feel the same
300 days of sunshine and virtually no rain

There's no Fall color to witness I've heard it said
And lack of water wilts the plants til they look dead
And though they call them rivers, they're as dry as a bone
Why in the world would you want to call this home?

Native plants absent of leaves, but plenty of spines
That puncture your skin if you pay them no mind
Venomous creatures, poisonous with their bite
Carnivores looking for a meal both day and night

No grass to paint the landscape a luscious green
Only rocks, cactus, and brown for miles to be seen
Lifeless desert extending to the distant sky
What kind of people would want to live here and why?

And yet when you take a closer look at this place
You realize there's so much more on which to base
Your judgment of this area's seeming adversity
And when you do, you'll discover its amazing diversity

The flatlands where nothing seems to live and grow
Come alive with wildflowers from the melting snow
Seeds that have been dormant for months on end
Suddenly spring to life and paint the barren land

The ever-changing mountains majestically rise
To complement each sunset and each sunrise
Dark and foreboding as the storms roll through
Green and misty with the morning dew

The stately saguaro adds to this glorious setting
Arms raised to heaven in supplicant feting
Standing guard year after year on the mountainside
Here when man was born; still here when he died

Covering like a magnificent umbrella this wondrous land
The stars and planets that have so intrigued man
The clear blue skies by day become the canvas at night
We become insignificant in this universe of light

There are the animals—some you've never known
We are so blessed they call this area home
The bobcat, mountain lion, javelina, and quail
They're not just here; they walk our trails

They make us aware of our caretaker role
Their beauty inspires us deep down in our soul
The deer, the rabbit, the coyote and more
Here in Arizona they're all at our back door

We have the canyons, both small and grand
Carved in the granite by God's own hand
Nature has shaped the rocks in their crimson hue
Each time we gaze their way, they're different, new

You'll often hear the phrase, "Valley of the Sun"
But Arizona doesn't end there; only begun
Both snowballs and swimming in your daily play
Where you can golf and ski, all in the same day

So, when someone tells you the desert's a waste
I hope you'll bring them here and give them a taste
Of a land that's as varied as the weather can be
A land uniquely gifted with amazing diversity.

Standing Tall

I'm a saguaro, straight and tall
Too young to have any arms at all
But when they develop, then I shall raise
Them to the heavens in supplicant praise

I'm not a bush, a flower, or vine
I'm unique, different, one of a kind
I don't resemble anything like a tree
A freak of nature, that be me

I flourish in soil where nothing else will grow
Majestically stand for eons though
Provide sanctuary for birds and such
But you humans just better not touch

I can go without water for nearly a year
As a desert dweller, I have no peer
When the monsoon comes, I swell with pride
Yet never burst from the water inside

I survive whether temps freeze or boil
Blessed by the Lord, I grow even in rocky soil
I stand the test of wind, rain, and snow
Here when you arrived; still here when you go

Someday I'll have arms; now I'm just a thumb
But considering all my gifts, that's enough for some
I'm looking forward to the day when my arms sprout
And I can thank the Lord for what I'm all about.

2
Charities

In today's world, it seems that more and more we want to rely on our government to be our safety net, and every day they prove they are incapable of doing so effectively. It's the volunteer effort that fills in the holes, and many of these charities, who are almost completely reliant on volunteers, are doing absolutely amazing work. Without them, many hurting people in our area would fall through the cracks. These two poems highlight two such charities that are offering a lifeline for those in desperate need, IMPACT of Southern Arizona and SaddleBrooke Community Outreach's Kids' Closet. Ronald Reagan once said, "We can't help everyone, but everyone can help someone." That certainly would be an appropriate mantra for the volunteers at these two charities.

IMPACT
Providing a Lifeline in Southern Arizona

The raging waters were everywhere, pulling me down
I had no idea which way was up or which way was down
And as I was about to go under for the very last time
There it was right in front of me, a lifeline

A complete stranger was standing there on the shore
Someone I didn't know and hadn't ever met before
He threw out a line and I clutched it in my hand
And with just a little help I was safely on land

Isn't this a metaphor for what happens to some?
One day we have everything; the next day none
We're struggling to make ends meet; to just get by
Who will bring us safely to shore and why?

We are not helpless, this you must understand
We just need that stranger with a helping hand
Be there to throw us a line, we'll do the rest
We'll swim as hard as we can and we'll both be blessed

Impact of Southern Arizona is changing lives in just this way
It's not welfare they're providing but an assist each day
It's a lifeline to help us make it on our own
Maybe to balance our budget or stay in our home

Maybe our health prevents us from getting out
And having meals delivered is what it's all about
Maybe there are too many bills and financial bumps
So that help with food or clothes gets us through the month

Maybe we have to learn something for the very first time
So we can do things ourselves and save dollars in kind
Maybe it's programs to deal with our children's despair
So they can go on with their lives much better prepared

Maybe it's a place where our seniors can rest and have fun
Knowing in doing so they're not the only ones
There are new life skills at which we need to be proficient
Our goal is not handouts, but to become self sufficient

This organization, Impact, is changing lives every day
And you can be part of it in so many ways
Won't you give them a call and donate money or time
They're awaiting your call at 825-0009.

Waiting To Smile

From all over the globe the volunteers come
The overriding qualification a great big heart
Yet the only reward when their work is done
Is the children's joyous faces as they depart

It's called Kids' Closet for it's all about clothes
Meant for kids whose families can't buy their own
Apparel available from their head to their toes
An outreach program like you've never known

Children of all ages and sizes; need the common thread
Picking out hats, shirts and jeans—all of it free
When they look in the mirror, not a word need be said
Though it's not unusual to hear "Look at me!"

This organization, though hardly noticeable at the start
Now clothes 2500 kids each Spring and Fall
It's a labor of love, straight from the heart
And over 200 volunteers now heed the call

So, if you're in search of real meaningful time
Wondering what you, with so little skill, could do
Come join us in the wardrobe line
There's a child waiting to smile just for you.

3
Commentary

Our world is changing and, mostly, not for the better. There seems to be no middle ground and we've strayed from the roots and heritage that made this country great. There is no easy answer, but I think if we can somehow return to the basics of God and family, we will have made tremendous strides.

In Vino, Veritas

Have you ever noticed when strangers get together
Conversation just seems to bog down under the pressure
There are awkward pauses and moments of nothing said
Not lively discussion, but a deafening silence instead

Then you come out with that first glass of wine
Conversation drifts as to whether you'd rate it a 10 or a 9
Finally, you have something to talk about, white or red
And you start to get that relaxed feeling in your head

You talk about the vineyard and the pleasant bouquet
The kind of grape—merlot, sangiovese or cabernet
Is the wine light and airy or full bodied and rich
And would it be better if it was cooled just a titch

That first glass is followed by one or two more
Uninhibited stories begin to flow by the score
You discover little details about each other you never knew
And the intriguing tales revealed just seem to accrue

Wine is the truth serum that loosens the tongue
And it works on the old as well as the young
There's an expression summarizing what this is all about
"In vino, veritas"—in wine, the truth will out

So be careful when you're invited to imbibe
Don't allow the evening to take you for a ride
It's a truth serum that may come with a cost
Don't be done in by "in vino, veritas."

Stroke of the Pen

If I could change the world with a stroke of the pen
I can think of a thousand places where I'd begin
The list is not exhaustive, but maybe it's a start
And we can make it happen with just a change of heart

When someone approaches, we'd hold open the door
And we'd say please and thank you a whole lot more
Courtesy, the forgotten word, would become common again
How you played the game would matter more than a win

God and family would be restored to their rightful place
We'd no longer twit and text, but converse face to face
Dinner would be a family occasion as in days of yore
And we'd really reach out to the hungry and poor

Love thy neighbor would not apply just to those next door
And we'd not be judged by our appearance or the clothes we wore
The preferred hand gesture would be two thumbs vertically thrust
And the me generation would become the generation of us

Video games and cell phones would have restricted use
Failing in school would have no acceptable excuse
Teachers would not be baby sitters or parents by day
And parents would hold their child accountable in every way

Road rage would not be instigated by blaring horn
Driver courtesy would become the new norm
Drugs would not be a problem because we'd educate
That they're the root of violence, destruction, and hate

Wars would become a thing of the past as would the pain
With so much more to lose than there would be to gain
Sectarian battles would mercifully come to an end
When we learned working together brought great dividends

Movies would be less violent and not permeated with sex
And four-letter words would not be standard text
The notion that what was once taboo is now OK
Would be replaced by absolutes for most of the gray

Our leaders would be civil and compromise reign
With much less concern for the re-election campaign
Our politicians would respond to questions direct
Not indulge us with non-answers, politically correct

Lawsuits would not be frivolous, with lawyers in line
We'd work out our differences with dialogue and time
The media would follow the story, not just dig up dirt
Concerned about who it affects and how much will it hurt

We'd restore Jesus to the center of all we do
Christmas and Easter—yes, but the rest of the year too
Merry Christmas wouldn't fall to Happy Holidays
And we'd study the Bible to learn Jesus' ways

Our litmus test, whether Gentile or Jew
Would be the Bible and what Jesus would do
His Word would be our instruction book, our guide
And we'd know why He lived and why He died

Obviously, it's not that simple, this stroke of the pen
But don't you think it's time we begin?
Otherwise, we're no better than animals who eat their young
And we'll pay dearly for the things we've done

So let's start today with an act randomly kind
With absolutely no benefit or reward in mind
Pay it forward with style and grace
And we'll help make this world a better place.

When Did The Rose Petals Fall To Earth?

When did the rose petals fall to earth
When did we lose our innocence
Where's the joy in just playing the game
In losing, why do we need someone to blame

Where have all our leaders gone
Where are the Washingtons and Lincolns
Is there no one who will stand his ground
Even when his approval rating is down

Where did the values we used to live by go
Common sense, morality, and family
When did our possessions equal success
Why does our lifestyle come with such stress

Why do we all become Americans when under attack
Then become divided again when the threat has passed
When did politically correct become a religion
Can't we back off our sensitivity just a smidgeon

Where have honesty and truth gone
When did fraud replace hard work to get ahead
When did law suits become so common place
Instead of talking things out face to face

Where did the simpler times of our youth go
When we played ball on a field instead of a screen
Why are so many of our heroes no heroes at all
Why are we not surprised when they finally fall

Would the Founding Fathers even recognize our country today
When did guns become the answer to every dispute
Why is the smallest accomplishment filled with hyperbole
And why can't we have success with a touch of humility

The world has changed all right and not for the better
Is there any way to return to what we once were
Or are we too far gone to have any hope at all
The solution just too difficult and too far down the hall

I think God gave us the answer oh so long ago
It's now in a box somewhere or covered in dust
Open up His Word; you'll find it exciting and new
Because following what it says is long overdue.

4
Inspirational

   Whatever we accomplish in life or whatever good we do for others usually has at its root a healthy dose of inspiration. Some of us, me included, search most of our lives to find true meaning—what are we here for? In my case, and maybe in yours, God has answered that question. Even if you're not a believer, maybe these poems will play some small part in your finding that calling and providing inspiration for you.

1st Corinthians Love

Words straight from the Bible, provoking thought
Defining what love is and what love is not
All laid out there in 1st Corinthians 13
Distilled to its essence; what it really means

Love is patient; love is kind
Slow, considerate, understanding comes to mind
Love does not boast or fill itself with pride
A humble heart cannot be denied

Love is not rude or seeking only self
It doesn't begin and end with trophies on the shelf
It is not easily angered; keeps no record of wrongs
Quickly suppresses flare-ups with a song

Love does not embrace evil, but rejoices in truth
Lies and deception abandoned in youth
Love always trusts, protects, and perseveres
Starts out small, but grows with the years

And as the years pass, only three things remain
But they're all we need to be sustained
Sent from our Father, straight from above
Faith, hope, and love but the greatest is love

So when our love is challenged in new ways
And we're not able to return to the good ole days
When our options seem to be way too few
Let's ask ourselves, "what would Jesus do?"

A Call to Action

Numbered are our days
Sands rush through the hourglass
Time is short to change our ways
Years ahead defer to years past

Without exception all men are lost
Only one way leads to eternal worth
The River Jordan we all must cross
And leave our material wealth here on earth

Time is wasting; listen, be still
His voice will whisper in your ear
Exhorting you to submit to His will
The days pass; His Spirit is near

Life doesn't have to end when we leave this earth
Jesus gave us a path to eternity with Him
Accept the Holy Spirit, an exciting new birth
And ask for forgiveness for all your sins

The call has gone out to change our behavior
The Day of Judgment is around the bend
Take action today to make Him Lord and Savior
And begin your life anew with Him!

A Poet's Rendition of the 23rd Psalm

Lord, you are my shepherd; I'm but a sheep
You are Master, God of the Universe, and King
All I have to do is my faithfulness keep
And I shall not be in need of anything

When my soul is restless, my heart in pain
You lead me to the still waters and I drink deep
You give me time to catch my breath and regain
That sense of peace and serenity I seek

Even Death Valley cannot have its way
I fear nothing or no one with You at my side
I turn to the power of your staff each day
Humble myself to You and cast out my pride

When I'm hungry, You serve me a gourmet dinner
My enemies watch, powerless to Your grace
You lift my head; make me feel like a winner
And the blessings flow all over the place

Your beauty and love are always there for me
I give thanks for each day that's free of strife
You made a promise; I've been set free
And I'll dwell in your house the rest of my life.

A Poet's Alternate Rendition of the 23rd Psalm

The Lord is my shepherd, my rock
I'm content to be one of His flock
He's always there to lead me; I know His voice
I'm compelled to follow, I have no choice

I shall never be in want nor want more
As long as Christ is there to go before
I trust the Good Shepherd in all His ways
He will provide for me, forgive me, and amaze

He makes me lie down in pastures green
He quiets my fears, seen and unseen
The presence of the Master fills my soul
I can release all my worries to His control

He leads me beside the waters still and deep
I'm at peace as one of His sheep
He guides me in the Way, the path of right
The lamp at my feet unmistakable and bright

Even in Death's shadow I have no fear
My Lord's comforting presence is always near
His authority is unquestioned; I have to obey
I'm under His protection tomorrow and today

He prepares a grand table just for me
Right there in front of my worst enemy
As His honored guest I am all aglow
The blessings are so numerous they overflow

Surely, my lot will be goodness and love
Directly from the Heavenly Father above
He will not leave my side, now or ever
And I shall dwell in His house forever.

Circle of Life

Just separate pieces of the puzzle, body and soul
Til God joins them together to make one whole
And a unique person is created at this moment in time
Even though the birth itself is further down the line

The writhing, squirming infant emerges from the womb
The proud father cheering the arrival from across the room
This completely helpless one can do nothing on his own
But does add to the happiness quotient of this loving home

Baby followed on by toddler, inquisitiveness beyond compare
If you don't want your "pretty" broken, better not leave it there
It's that time to explore everything that's within the grasp
Only recently learned to walk, but still gets there fast

The pre-teen years, a period of rapid learning and growth
Still leaning heavily on mom and dad; needing them both
Virtually no awareness of the soul through this time
A happy period; simple concerns; the world looks fine

The teen period, a time of change, see what unfurls
Emotions, raging hormones and yes, first awareness of girls
Discovery, peer pressure, and depression all rolled into one
Awareness of the soul is there but only barely begun

Young adulthood brings with it new challenges and fears
Which route, college or a trade on which to build a career?
Beginning to once again understand how little we know
And God keeps strengthening that thing called soul

Then she comes and life's never quite the same
There's nothing she wouldn't do, even change her name
We're standing at the altar, her hand in mine
What lies ahead will only be told by the passage of time

It's not long before beautiful children come along
There's pressure but it gives in to joy; life's a song
The years pass so quickly we can hardly believe
They're all grown up—adults themselves and ready to leave

And all this time God's Spirit speaks as never before
There's push back but it's a voice that can't be ignored
That thing he placed inside, what we call soul
Makes us this unique individual, that we know

The autumn of our years has finally arrived
We're thankful for each day given; each day alive
We're concerned with the body, but much more with the soul
Our focus on the spiritual intensifies as we grow old

Once more we are dependent, childlike, a wretch
Simple tasks we once took for granted are now a stretch
We need help walking, eating; understanding's a chore
Hair is thinning and fading is our memory of all things before

Our body and soul, once joined are separated again
The body goes to ashes; the soul to Him
And with this soul crossing to the other side
We complete the circle of life to be by His side.

Enough

Blessed beyond what we can describe
Sufficiency evident, if conscience be our guide
So not wishing you more irrelevant stuff
What I wish for you is I wish you enough

Enough cloudy, dreary, and rainy days
That you revel in the sun and bask in its rays
Enough failure in business and other relations
That success in either brings wild elation

Enough ache in your step that when the hurt's done
You cherish the moment you can freely run
Enough affliction in your day-to-day livin'
That good health is not viewed as a given

Enough wonder at the nighttime universe
That you believe God's Word, chapter and verse
Enough adult decisions, made and filed
That you delight in showing your inner child

Enough scars from skirmishes that never cease
That you can truly celebrate a lasting peace
Enough love lost in the dating run
That you recognize and idolize "The One"

Enough grind-and-sweat labor every day
That you can devote the same energy to when you play
Enough enemies, real or perceived
That investing in friendships is what you believe

Enough fear and trepidation in all things new
That you accomplish more than you thought you could do
Enough cold, lonely, and sleepless nights
That you can take "warm and cuddly" to new heights

Victory is much sweeter after a resounding defeat
Love found after love lost is hard to beat
That's why some challenge is good; times that are tough
And why my wish for you is I wish you enough.

How Does Your Garden Grow?

We prepare the soil painstakingly to ensure success of the seed
    It is nourished with fertilizer, water, and the sun's glow
    Then one day it appears—a beginning, a tender reed
    Others follow poking through the ground row by row

    Looking across the garden, not a weed can be seen
    Just intentional plants sprouting without interference
    Turning the land to an orderly, purposeful sea of green
    There is joy as each new plant makes its grand appearance

The joy is short-lived, however; things are beginning to change
    Other seeds are germinating and they're not to sweeten
    These new plants are aggressively expanding their range
    And the Garden of Eden is becoming the Garden of Weeden

    We have many choices on how to rid the garden of weeds
We can pull them, hoe them out, or treat them with Weed-B-Gone
    It's hard work taking care of all the garden's needs
But if we do it right, the vegetables will flourish and it won't be long

    Doesn't our own life parallel the garden in so many ways?
    At first, we're so clean and innocent, a beautiful child to behold
    Then sin creeps into our life, growing stronger each day
    And if we do nothing, it takes over and we spin out of control

    But if we tend to our garden and stamp out the spiritual weeds
    Making good choices and resisting every temptation
    Listening to God's Word and standing tall in word and deeds
    We'll become a light in the dark and a source of inspiration

    So, the question you might have heard before,
        how does your garden grow?
Is it untended, overgrown, and in need of attention and prayers
Is today the day you go after those weeds with your spiritual hoe
There's a Father in Heaven who's watching and He really cares.

I Woke Up This Morning and I'm Not Dead

What shall I do with this day that lies before
What adventure awaits as I walk out the door
I hope I'm ready for whatever lies ahead
Because I woke up this morning and I'm not dead

Will I meet someone I've never met before
Or will it be an old friend from way back yore
I hope I'll learn something new, as it's been said
Because I woke up this morning and I'm not dead

Will it be some kind of calamity that's in store
Or some kind of victory causing my spirit to soar
Maybe I'll delve into a book that I've never read
Because I woke up this morning and I'm not dead

Will I be a blessing to someone who needs my help
Bringing satisfaction like I've never felt
I hope I don't just lay there, lounging in bed
Because I woke up this morning and I'm not dead

Will it be time with family—fun and so well spent
Will it start with a quiet prayer heaven sent
The opportunities are limitless, a to zed
Because I woke up this morning and I'm not dead

I know God is there and will direct my path
I pray that He showers me with love, not His wrath
If I but listen to His calling, I know I'll be led
Because I woke up this morning and I'm not dead

Maybe the day will be routine, nothing new coming my way
In any case, I still expect it to be a wonderful day
I plan to take it one day at a time, not look ahead
Because I woke up this morning and I'm not dead

Will the world be a better place when this day is done
Will I bring into someone's dreary life a little fun
I hope my focus is not on me, but others instead
Because I woke up this morning and I'm not dead

I'm waiting on you, Lord; what's your plan
My life today is completely in your hands
Father, give me this day, my daily bread
Because I woke up this morning and I'm not dead.

In Full Bloom

The Dogwood—serene beauty in full bloom
God's caring, loving touch realized
In its presence, peaceful solitude looms
And anxiety, depression and anguish dies.

The Dogwood is not master of its own
Boldly and brashly proclaiming its flair
Rather preferring not to stand alone
But simply adding glorious strokes to what's already there.

Incredible isn't it that once only a seed
With love and nurturing and care
It poked through the earth, became the reed
And continued to develop and grow from there.

Next a sapling, at once vulnerable and frail
Needing staking and tethered support
To protect it from the whims of nature,
Wind, rain, hail –things of that sort.

Then, one Spring, there is the breakthrough
A single blossom is followed by several more
A small beginning, hardly worth the view
But a mere hint of the potential in store.

In Springs to follow, the sapling becomes the tree
Developing branches seek new paths to the sun
Flowers everywhere for the world to see
And gloriously, God's work is done.

Deb, you're so much like that Dogwood
We hope our love carried you through the growing pains
We hope we supported you like we should
And helped you cope with the winds of change.

We've watched you grow from that tiny sapling
To the wonderful young lady you've become
Branching out into new worlds and grappling
With all challenges; backing down from none.

And, like the Dogwood, you don't need to be the star
But your presence adds immensely to any group
You're very content being who you are
Working with others to complete the loop.

That glimmer of potential's now in full bloom
For today you graduate from SMSU
Finishing in style, as a Magna Cum
As parents, we're proud as we can be of you.

Like the trees behind the Dogwood, we'll always be here
Supporting, protecting, shaping and such
As you meet the challenges of each new year.
You're a special daughter and we love you very much.

In Full Bloom Revisited

The Dogwood tree– serene beauty in full bloom
God's caring, loving touch realized
In its presence, peaceful solitude looms
And anxiety, depression and anguish dies.

The Dogwood is not master of its own
Boldly and brashly proclaiming its flair
Rather preferring not to stand alone
But simply adding glorious strokes to what's already there.

Incredible isn't it that once only a seed
With love and nurturing and care
It poked through the earth, became the reed
And continued to develop and grow from there.

Next a sapling, at once vulnerable and frail
Needing staking and tethered support
To protect it from the whims of nature,
Wind, rain, hail –things of that sort.

Then, one Spring, there is the breakthrough
A single blossom is followed by several more
A small beginning, hardly worth the view
But a mere hint of the potential in store.

In Springs to follow, the sapling becomes the tree
Developing branches seek new paths to the sun
Flowers everywhere for the world to see
And gloriously, God's work is done.

Hopefully our children are like that Dogwood
And our love carries them through the growing pains
That we support them the way parents should
And help them cope with the winds of change.

Nurturing them as they grow from that tiny sapling
To the wonderful young men and women they can become
Branching out into new worlds and grappling
With all challenges; backing down from none.

Teach them, like the Dogwood, they don't need to be the star
Their presence alone adds immensely to any group
Tell them to be content just being who they are
Working with others to complete the loop.

Like the trees behind the Dogwood stand firm in support
Give them the belief they can reach for the moon
Trust them to their ambition and dreams; don't cut them short
And that glimmer of potential will reach full bloom.

It's The Heart

Not the brain
Not the intellectual exercise of a genius IQ
Great minds often achieve worldly fame
But can't imagine how to be born anew

Not the eyes
What we see can be so deceiving
Satan in many forms, master of disguise
But faith in the unseen can bring true believing

Not the mouth
Treachery lies in every corner, said and unsaid
Words better smothered, find their way out
Dispensing not compassion, but distress instead

Not the ears
The truth is evident, but we don't listen
The Holy Spirit communicates, but we don't hear
Our internal receiver just seems to be missing

Not the circumcision
That under Jewish law was such a part
Rather an internal change was Paul's vision
A circumcision alright, but one of the heart

The heart is where it all begins
Is it a hardened and sealed off place
Or has it rejected Satan's call to sin
And freely accepted God's amazing grace?

When the Holy Spirit calls your name
And you're not sure just where to start
Invite Him in; accept the change
He will lead you if you just open your heart.

Pandora's Box

It's a legend of Greek mythology that people know even today
And they would tell you the story is irrelevant in so many ways
You know the one where Pandora opens the box or jar
And all the evils of the world are released near and far

Death, destruction, perversion, murder, and rape
Lies, gossip, envy, and greed, they and more all escaped
Closing the box left only one thing to help us cope
Way down at the bottom was the blessing of hope

When we look at our world today these evils are all there
They seem to be growing in strength, pervasive everywhere
The nightly news is full of tragedy, hopelessness, and fall
Where can we run to; can we get away from it all?

Where does the answer lie; can we change and learn?
Can these evils somehow be put back in the urn?
Or are we relegated to committing the same old sins
Is hope still in that box and can it be revived again?

There is a place where we can find the hope we need
It's not in a box or jar, but it is hope's only seed
It's the Bible and its message is even more pertinent today
The One who died for us is ready to listen if we just pray

Politicians don't have the answers; the government is broken
Follow the words in red and how clearly they're spoken
Our Lord is coming to restore His kingdom, He told us so
And that promise is the only hope we need to know

Yes, Pandora is just a fable, but the hope can still resonate
The evils of this world can be put back; it's not too late
Jesus told us "I am the life, the truth, and the way"
Only He can bring the hope that we crave today.

Simmer in Prayer

Solar tea is made with water and tea caressed by the sun
Its essence is released as a gentle, unhurried process is run
You cannot brew a proper tea with a satisfying taste
Using extremely hot water and tea made in haste

Likewise my Master is at work and I'm simmering as His tea
He has many different ways to bring out the essence of me
It's a slow process as He teaches me the wonders of Him
Removing the bitter taste that comes with the intrusion of sin

Sometimes I try to take over the process, brew my own me
The result of this free will is expected and easy to foresee
This brew, when finished, is rancid; not at all drinkable
And going my own way completely unthinkable

I am steeped in His love and slowly I'm beginning to see
That He has just the right process for the flavor of me
And all I have to do to make me a brew beyond compare
Is go to the Lord in worship and simmer in prayer.

Steady Your Brother's Ladder

The ladder is there before us
And from early childhood we begin the climb
Better student, better athlete, recognition a must
Pulling ourselves up, one rung at a time

There's college, certainly one of prestige
We need that plaque on the wall when the job's done
Our pursuit of excellence never does cease
And we pull ourselves up another rung

Our career begins and we play the game so well
Promotions follow; victories are won
Bigger house, fancier car, anyone can tell
We've pulled ourselves up several more rungs

Climbing ever higher, we swell with pride
Conversation centers around successful me
We arrange our trophies, side by side
The money god just won't set us free

Then, one day as we enter the autumn of our days
We wonder quietly, what has our life really meant?
Why the emptiness, what's the legacy we've saved
And for our children, what message was sent

Then, without warning it hits like a bolt heaven sent
Why didn't we see it; it's so clear what's the matter
We're not satisfied with the rapid ascent
Because we've busied our self with the wrong ladder

Ditch the ladder of self; steady another to prevent his fall
What can you do to help your brother climb a rung
You know what you need to do so heed the call
And you'll find meaning in what you've done.

That Changed Everything

To some you were just a baby conceived like many before
To the Pharisees, you weren't the one they were looking for
You didn't fit the mold of the warrior, the all-conquering King
But when you arose from the dead that changed everything

To some you were just a carpenter, plying his trade
Handiwork creations perhaps proudly displayed
May have thought these were the only skills you'd bring
But when you arose from the dead that changed everything

To some you were just another prophet of zealous fame
One of those with a following, but no lasting name
Most couldn't imagine you could be the real thing
But when you arose from the dead that changed everything

To some you were just a preacher with tricks up your sleeve
Nothing more than a magician some would believe
At times even your apostles would not your praises sing
But when you arose from the dead that changed everything

But now we know you came to earth us sinners to save
Death would not have its way in that earthly grave
And now we know you were truly the Messiah, the King
Because when you arose from the dead that changed everything.

The Big Room

As I stood there in this enormous room, feeling terrified and small
I looked around and couldn't be sure it was a room at all
The walls were more like barricades of light and went on forever
My heart was pounding and I hadn't felt like this, ever

Then I looked up, saw this big board and gasped at the display
There for all to see were my sins from birth until today
They were scrolling across the screen in an endless show
The ones from just yesterday and ones so long ago

The sins of my life were all there in excruciating detail
The times I swore, lied, and cheated so as not to fail
The times I gossiped about others, including friends
The people I offended and never made amends

The people who were different that I ignored without a thought
The times I celebrated stealing something and not getting caught
The times I drank too much and justified going wild
The times, as a grownup, I acted like a child

The times I grumbled because things weren't going my way
Forgetting to thank God for each and every day
Turning away instead of helping those in need
Worshipping the money god with unabashed greed

Coveting the material possessions of my neighbor next door
His big house, fancy car, bank account and more
Not stopping to realize I had also been immensely blessed
No matter, the grass was always greener I guess

The times I refused to let humility be my guide
Bragging about accomplishments with unmitigated pride
Believing that somehow it was all under my control
And that I didn't need God to make me whole

The list went on and on and on until I could look no more
How was it someone knew everything about me right to the core?
I thought I had lived a good life, a good person all right
So why was I ready to run; ready to take flight?

My face turned red, my palms began to sweat, my eyes to tear
All of my friends were watching with me, worsening my fear
I began to choke, the breaths coming short and strained
Where was I and why was it so out of this world and strange?

Then I saw Him in the distance, dressed in white and all aglow
What was the penalty He had for me? I deserved it I know
I remember reading that death is the wage of sin
I could not speak; no place to hide, no place to begin

As I was about to say I'm sorry for everything I'd done
He opened His arms and said "Welcome home, son"
Tears welled up in my eyes and I fell to my knees
I knew it was too late, but I said, "Lord, forgive me please."

Then I noticed what looked like blood flowing down the screen
And as it did, it was erasing all my transgressions we had just seen
I stared in disbelief at what I did not understand
Then it dawned on me—the blood of the Son of Man!

And then they were there, thousands of angels, that is
They encircled us closely and I knew they were His
The songs of joy they were singing were like nothing I'd heard
The lyrics, though, came straight from the Word

I was dumbfounded as I looked one last time at the board
And all I could get out was "Thank you, Lord"
For the screen was blank, the sins were lost
Except for these words "Debt paid on the cross"

Then I was awake, was it a vision or just a dream?
The message was so vivid, though, I know what it means
It's a reminder that I am found where once I was lost
And that He gave it all up for me there on the cross.

Thorns Always Come With The Rose

We have such a fascination with the rose
It's above all other flowers in poetry and prose
Its beauty represents love in its purest form
And we love it in every way, except for the thorns

So why does the rose always seem to have a bite
May I suggest that suffering is part of the rite
The sacrifice to be made; the pain to record
That loveliness we celebrate is pain's reward

The rose is a metaphor for life; that's a fact
Words are spoken that we can never take back
Thoughtlessness and conflict are the thorns that get in the way
And we forget to say I love you each and every day

Love that lasts is rarely captured in a day
There are hurdles and challenges along the way
There is hurt and anguish as we walk through the years
Moments of bliss are there, but so are the tears

But if we can navigate this treacherous road
The rewards are great for the seeds we've sowed
We'll find a love that grows stronger each day
And nothing, absolutely nothing can ruin the bouquet

Love always comes with the forgiveness that sooths
The beauty in all of us that makes the heart move
So take the thorns that puncture and scratch our being
With it comes the most beautiful rose you've ever seen.

Today is a Gift

Today is a gift
A blessing for sure
Will it be one to treasure
Or just another to endure?

Each day is an opportunity
The Lord has sent your way
Will you use it wisely
Or just let it slip away?

Time is racing forward
This day will soon be done
Will you fill the fleeting minute
With a full sixty seconds run?

Will you be receptive
To what God has in store?
Or will you go your own way
Like so many times before?

Will you appreciate the beauty
Of flowers, mountain, and brook?
Or will you be so engrossed
You fail to even look?

Will you encourage a friend
Not wasting another minute?
Or will you forget how they enrich your life
And how glad you are they're in it?

Will you be a blessing
To someone less fortunate than you?
Or will you just walk away
Convinced there's nothing you can do?

Will you look to the heavens
And contemplate God's awesome power
Be grateful that He walks with you
Each second, each minute, each hour?

Will today be the day
When you say "Yes, Lord, Yes"
I'm following You
With a heart full of thankfulness?

What if somehow you knew
That today was your last day?
Would you have a list of regrets
About what you failed to do or say?

Don't let this day pass
The sand is trickling through
Today is a gift
From our Lord to you.

Traveling The Back Roads

We travel the freeways at breakneck speed
It's just part of the modern-day stampede
We just can't wait to get wherever we're going
Is it important or just our impatience showing?

But aren't we missing a lot as we race along?
Where's the symphony, the ballet, and the song?
Can we really appreciate the artist's brush
As we immerse ourselves in this headlong rush?

Of course, the freeways are but an analogy
For this fast-paced life we lead, this insanity
We have no stop or pause button; no way to rewind
We're just so afraid we'll fall hopelessly behind

Technology is what fuels this unrelenting style
Everything at the touch of our fingers, all the while
Limitless information available across our phones
So connected in every way and yet so alone

Maybe once in awhile we should take the back road
Dump our cares into that electronic download
Take a peaceful stroll and ditch the phone
Amble the shores of a placid lake; skip a stone

Ever notice that the grass is green and the sky is blue?
Take a look around; these moments are precious few
The world comes to life as you slow your pace
The wonder of nature right there for you to taste

Find your place where quiet and reflection reign
You'll find there's a lot to be learned in the slow lane
Early morning hour on the patio or under a tree
Creativity spawns on the sea of tranquility

God won't try to compete with our worldly din
He'll just wait for you to be still and tune in
Just like it's impossible to appreciate bird or flower
You won't be able to find God at 70 miles per hour

So locate that back road of life anyway you can
It's waiting, calling to take you by the hand
And when you do, you'll find a peace like you've never known
And God will be waiting there patiently, on His throne.

Twelve Ordinary Men

They were just twelve ordinary men
Living out their lives in the simplest way
You wouldn't have chosen any of them
Blue collar workers we'd call them today

Several fishermen, a fanatic, and a tax man
What could we really expect them to do?
Either despised or of no account back then
What they were capable of no one knew

They had the greatest teacher in the world
But they couldn't grasp the essence of his mission
They listened but it was as if they never heard
These were not men of great speech or vision

They had intensive training for three years
And yet, at the crucial moment, they were lost
Denying they even knew him, they gave in to their fears
And watched in horror as their leader died on the cross

But God had yet to unleash his extraordinary power
They had no idea of what was coming; what was in store
The Holy Spirit would be sent at the appointed hour
And their ordinary lives would be ordinary no more

Like a tiny flame quickly becomes a raging fire when given air
These twelve took the Gospel to the ends of the earth
Their Great Commission was no longer one of despair
It was as if they had experienced a second birth

Aren't we like the twelve—just ordinary folk after all
Struggling to make a living; trying to survive
But not really living until we receive the call
And take up a higher reason to be alive

God has a purpose for each of us; a reason, a goal
The power of the Holy Spirit will show us the way
Follow the calling as the twelve did so long ago
And ordinary can still become extraordinary today.

Wildflower

The seed finds its resting place where it can
Carried there by animal, wind, or man
It might find fertile soil or only rock
Obligated, though, to wait in dry dock

Then one day the rains come pouring down
The transformation begins below the ground
Seedling pokes through at the appointed hour
And in all its glory bursts forth the wildflower

One is followed by two; then quickly a score
In short order, they fill an acre or more
Red, golden, and blue compose the scheme
We stand in awe, marveling at the scene

Christians are formed in much the same way
A seed is planted by someone one day
It may or may not find a receptive soul
A hardened heart cannot accept the role

Then one day lightning strikes a spiritual chord
Maybe the right person or just the right word
Maybe it's a tragedy or a friend's advice
That sprouts a new believer in Christ

Unsure of his faith, just a fledgling at first
But strengthened by God and Bible verse
The Holy Spirit comes and the growth's complete
Like the wildflower, an aroma pure and sweet

But that's only the beginning of this odyssey
Disciple follows disciple in this new ministry
The brothers meet often to fellowship and pray
And strengthen each other in following the Way

Their numbers grow daily as others want to be
With the Lord, as He promised, for all eternity
And when the Lord looks down from his Heavenly tower
It's more pleasing to Him than any wildflower.

You and I

They were just a group of fisherman
No skills to do the job at hand
But leaving the nest, He taught them to fly
And He can do the same for you and I

Not able to sing even the chorus
Or speak on the simplest theme?
If He can use a tax collector guy
I know He can use you and I

Have not the slightest gift of persuasion
Nor any ability to teach or lead?
The Twelve often asked themselves why
But they followed and so should you and I

Find it difficult to show compassion
Have no powers to console or heal?
The Twelve were connected to the Most High
And if we are, He can use you and I

Can't perform any miracles
You're not the one to spread the news?
If God can change Saul to Paul, then why
Would you think He cannot change you and I

One of God's greatest servants was slow of speech
Yet led his people out of Egypt to the Promised Land
He was obedient to God you cannot deny
We can trust and obey as well, you and I

We don't need to make a splash
Appear somewhere on the evening news
We don't need to be the conquering hero and die
God can use the little things from you and I

We don't have to be like the Twelve
With a legacy from 2000 years ago
We just have to accept the challenge and try
That's all God asks of us, you and I.

Your Guardian Angel

An old friend; a stranger with a good deed
A fortuitous change of events in time of need
Manifested to you in a variety of ways
I'm your Angel; guardian of your days.

A full bouquet when there was no seed
From the bondage of this world I have been freed
Through others, my powers oft displayed
I'm your Angel; guardian of your days.

Let this pin be a reminder I'll always be there
To pick you up when it seems no one cares
You might not even notice, so subtle my ways
But ever present I'll be, guarding your days.

5
Dogs

Dogs are God's gift to man. Just pay attention—they provide unconditional love regardless of how you treat them and they'll greet you when you come through the door as if you've been gone for days or weeks instead of hours. We can learn a lot from our dogs—joy, love, and trust just to name a few.

D.O.G., Delight of God

I come running when I hear the door
I'm so excited my feet leave the floor
I want to walk beside you whenever I can
I just want to be with you, that's my plan
When you lay down I want to cuddle in tight
I want you part of my routine, both day and night
I don't get bored with doing the same old things
I rely on you for food, for love, for everything
My love is not conditional on anything you do
If you treat me bad, I'm still there waiting for you
When you're out of my sight, depression sets in
Until you return and I'm all happy again
My emotions not hidden you understand
I'm overjoyed to feel the touch of your hand
My name and God's share the same letters
He created me to make your life so much better
To model a love that never varies, never ends
I'm His delight, your dog and faithful friend.

Joy in the Now

Comes enthusiastically when you call his name
No matter how many times, responds the same
Excitement he cannot contain, joy so sweet
Jumps out of his skin and dances on his feet

Dependent on his master for everything every day
Works hard to please him; happy to obey
Kisses on your hands, your ears, and feet
It's love he gives and love he seeks

Wants to be with you whatever you do, wherever you turn
Sad when you leave; ecstatic with your return
Makes us laugh when playtime rolls around
Picks us up when we're feeling down

His master is his love, his idol, his king
He's dependent on him for everything
His trust goes way beyond anything known
Depression sets in when he's on his own

Is life with our Master also a must?
No matter what, do we obey and trust?
Maybe God sent us the dog to show us how
To unconditionally love and find joy in the now.

6
Family and Friends

All animal life thrives on social interaction, and man is no different. Family and friends are the people in our lives with whom we have lasting relationships. We know everything about each other, we care for each other, and we would do anything for each other. Life would be empty and without meaning if they weren't there. These poems say some of the things many of us, myself included, have trouble saying face to face to the people who are most important in our lives.

A New Star in Heaven

There's a new star apparent in our nightly sky
Not as bright as some of the others but pleasing to the eye
It's not impressive with its size or shine
But its attraction is unmistakable, if sublime

This star is humble but will lure you like the butterfly
You'll come under its spell and won't know why
It just brings a sense of quiet confidence and peace
All the cares and worries of the day it will release

When this star shines, it's like an irresistible smile
And you just have to smile back all the while
Would that on earth we could affect others this way
And learn from what this star has to say

You'll see this star if you look to the East at night
Just as the moon rises, your spirit will rise at the sight
It brings a message from God, a message of hope
Whatever is bothering you, it will help you cope

There's a gentle nature about this star's display
That can be sensed even light years away
It will change your mood, even your inner being
You'll wonder why you're so affected by what you're seeing

Somehow this star is connected to all the rest
Maybe holding them together I would suggest
And you'll feel connected too as you hold your gaze
And realize the impact this star has on your days

Does this star have a name that we can call
Its place was reserved and sanctioned by God after all
I know there's only one name that fits truly
So here on earth we'll just call it Judy.

A Standing Ovation

For supporting your husband in his career
Subjugating your goals to his, year after year
Willingly allowing him to bask in the glory
While your behind-the-scenes work was the real story

For the way you cultured our children in the Christian way
Those values still entrenched to this very day
For how you tutored us that God is in control
And it matters not our own agenda or who we know

For being there for the children, grandchildren and all
Understanding the needs; not requiring a call
Caring for us when sick, boosting us when shattered
A willing listener to a friend, when that's all that mattered

For the way you reach out to the disadvantaged and poor
And welcome to the community people next door
For your gift of hospitality, an amazing craft
Bringing diversity together for a much needed laugh

For your thoughtfulness and unending kindness in deed
Reaching out to anyone where you see a need
First in line to share, time and resources to give
A shining example of what it means to really live

For the lives, over the years, you have touched
Reassuring words and kindred spirit meant so much
Your goodwill played forward in others' replies
Quietly your influence expands and multiplies

For much less achieved, we've seen great celebrations
Pomp and circumstance and standing ovations
For the things you do; the things you've done, we are awed
That's why we stand now, on your birthday, and applaud.

A Year Ago Today

A year ago today your wedding vows
What a wonderful snippet of life
We really treasure the memory now
Of you taking each other as husband and wife

Stargazers, candelabras, a new world found
Ceremony orchestrated from A to zitch
Debbie all radiant in her white satin gown
Everything proceeding without a hitch

Well, maybe that's stretching it just a tad
Seems a few keys were still in flux
Father of the bride steps out of a cab
Has anyone seen the best man's tux?

The penny in the shoe Dad couldn't figure out
Seems a little uptight and no one knows why
But Scott's relaxed and free of doubt
His jacket is closed and so is his fly

The little quirks and foibles aside
The ceremony is, at once, simple and grand
To Maderos' heartfelt renditions we cried
And beamed as you took each other's hand

Guests, they're many, a sell-out I'd say
Streaming in from every city and town
Miracle of miracles, on this special day
Scott's dad – we just couldn't keep him down

Stroll down the aisle, unity candles lit
Thoughts of the pastor, love pledges fair
A touching moment you have to admit
And ever so quickly, Mr. & Mrs. Mayer

Pictures to follow and the reception fling
Heart of St. Charles, party all night
We'll keep doing this hat and hula thing
Until we drop or get it right!

Yes, the usual traditions of the fete
Bouquet and garter toss, best man toast
The father of the bride will never forget
The song by Celine touched him most

In a few short hours, festivities no more
Off to the hotel and honeymoon cruise
Of this new son we're not so sure
Tuxedoed next day, but no socks or shoes

A year's gone by, in a heartbeat it seems
You've grown in love, kind of day by day
But, in those moments when you're in our dreams
We're still remembering a year ago today.

Always in My Heart

Things I should have said; things I should have done
Things never finished; things never begun
Things which could have been set right with just a word
Thoughts not aired; but rather inferred

Mistakes aplenty as I walked through this life
On the job training on how to love my wife
But as the years have passed, quickly I might add
What a wonderful learning experience I've had

You taught me how to live, laugh, and love
How to seek guidance from our Father above
The importance of God, family, and friends
Refresher course required every now and then

If I ever made you feel second best, that I regret
Because the best day of my life was the day we met
And when life's troubles start to pull me down
I need to remember you're the blessing I found

So if I ever neglected to put you first on my list
I would ask that you just remember this
Until the day we from this earth depart
You are always there, always in my heart.

Amazing Grace

We all know the girly girl stereotype
Makeup, short dresses, and fashion hype
Dolls, ribbons, lace and such
But not this girl, not so much

Grace is her own person that's for sure
Don't be bringing frills and bling around her
Love pink we've often heard it said
But not in her clothes, not even a thread

Sport shorts and tees are what she wears
Fashion, smashion, you think she cares?
Give her her pads and hockey stick
Have you ever even heard of a hat trick?

Her diet also fits an unconventional style
Setting those burgers and fries aside for awhile
Salads and brussel sprouts can make a perfect meal
And anytime of the day is right for cereal

Her teams are the Packers and LA Kings
She likes players who wear championship rings
Players who show some attitude and grit
Not the ones who surrender at the first hard hit

So, if you want to be her friend, better toughen up
Leave your girly stuff at home when you show up
Come play knee hockey with the boys upstairs
You're invited to mix it up if you even dare

And when she drives, whether motorbike or ATV
It's strictly fast and furious you're gonna see
Full throttle, pedal to the metal, that's her plan
You don't stand a chance, but catch her if you can

And yet, she's a gentle soul with a kind and generous heart
Someone you'll be drawn to right from the start
But be aware she has a black belt in Tae Kwon Do
She can break boards with her hands, just so you know

If you think she's one dimensional, better think again
This girl's smart and academically, plays to win
And we can't wait to see when the race of life is run
Not only what she does, but who she becomes

The world is her oyster and the sky's the limit
She's growing up so fast, kind of a New York minute
Whatever path she takes in life, she's bound to excel
Because that all-out spirit will serve her well

There's nothing we can say or do to earn our place
We just call it a gift from God, His amazing grace
And isn't that our Grace as well, amazing in every way
We're just so thankful she's with us each and every day.

Chandlers' Wedding Program

We look back now at the road we've run
Just a passing glance at trials overcome
For it's not the past, but the future we embrace
As we stand before you, face to face.

Our horizon limitless, spanning the sky
We begin this journey together, you and I
Our age of discovery and adventure, a whole new life
We step into it now, as husband and wife.

I'll look into your eyes and you into mine
And savor the love in this new lifeline
This day began with a brand new sun
So it will be with this life as one.

This day is fragile; soon it will end
And once vanished will not come again
This day is fleeting and when it slips away
No amount of money can buy back this day.

So, now as we take each other – you and me
We'll cherish this moment, so faithfully
For this day is fragile; soon it will end
This day when I marry my best friend.

Diamonds Are Forever

Last time together, it was 50 years of gold
Now we're all here, ten years more old
Our steps a little slower, our memory less clear
As we come to celebrate your diamond year.

Diamonds start out a mere lump of coal
No luster at all and worthless to hold
So too the marriage; not much at the start
But a packet of dreams and love from the heart.

Then, like the coal, a slow change does occur
As time and pressure, at God's hands insure
That what's created stands the test of time
Whether the diamond or a marriage divine.

As the diamond, the marriage blessed is a rock
Neither chipped nor scratched by life's hard knocks
It continues to shine in the darkest hour
And the love of two doubles its power.

Diamonds are forever I've heard them say
Surely your marriage is also that way
For you've always been able when times got tough
To look around and find the diamond in the rough.

And when the Lord calls to take you home
We know you won't be making the trip alone
You'll be coaching other couples at St. Peter's gate
How wonderful it can be with an eternal mate.

Emma — One of a Kind

A gift from God, unexpected, a surprise
And she's growing up right before our eyes
There's not any one thing by which she's defined
She's Emma and she's definitely one of a kind

She's sweet and loving, first and foremost
Can shake her booty better than most
An infectious smile that lights up any room
Knows all the words to the latest tunes

You can tell a lot about a person's character
By how she treats animals and how they react to her
Emma loves horses, dogs, any animal you can name
And she fusses over them all pretty much the same

Her exuberance is delightful and contagious
Fancy-free spirit can border on outrageous
A warm heart to everyone, stranger or friend
But if that sounds like weakness, better think again

She's sensitive and caring in a good way
But if you cross her, she'll make you pay
Because she'll stand her ground, have no doubt
If you bully her, she might punch your lights out

Started out with gymnastics, but now soccer's her game
Better come prepared or she'll put you to shame
Bubble wrap my broken wrist and I'll give it my all
You don't need hands to kick a soccer ball

Intensity is just part of her persona, OK?
Give her the ball if you're not making a play
And if you see her fall and wince in pain
Don't even think of taking her out of the game

If she has one weakness, it's being forgetful, distracted
It's a personality trait she'd like to have redacted
It's about the only thing for which she'll complain
"Why", you'll hear her say, "did I get dad's brain?"

Emma has so many strengths we know she'll go far
Whatever she does, she's destined to be a star
We're all watching for her life story to unwind
It will be incredible because she's one of kind.

Fifty Golden Years

50 Golden Years, somehow the time just flies
And during that time, you've faced the lows and the highs
But as you look forward and reminisce about the past
Isn't it curious how it's the joy, not the sadness, that lasts.

For while there were seemingly unanswerable questions
During the two world wars and the Great Depression
And there was, of course, the normal suffering and strife
So much dreaded, but such a part of life.

There were many more moments of happiness and bliss
Like the first time alone and that very first kiss
Like courtship, proposal and the wedding day
When you vowed to love each other the rest of the way.

And then there were the children, Joey the first
Who, being a boy, thought he surely was cursed
And so each night in his prayers and wishes
He'd ask for a sister who could do the dishes.

Now God's work takes time, you must understand
And it was eight years before the stork came again
To deliver Marie Antoinette to the door
And round out a loving family of four.

There are the memories of those child-rearing years
Of the hugs and kisses, the laughter and tears
Of the teenager who alternately sulks and rejoices
And you pray that you've taught them to make the right choices.

And finally adulthood, when the child leaves the nest
It's with mixed emotion that you wish them the best
For it's a special joy that even Dad can't hide
The tear in his eye as he gives away the bride.

God must have understood, in His masterful plan
The void that's created when the children disband
For the grandchildren that followed were not born of luck
Louise, Dennis, Lisa, Debbie and Chuck.

Grandchildren are really better than having your own
For you can love them and spoil them – then send them home
And what a wonderful way to stay young and alive
Trying to keep up with kids when you're fifty-five.

But not all pleasures of life around family revolve
There are other interests and challenges to solve
For Mom there were new culinary hights
With her lasagna, pizza and other Italian delights.

And for Dad there was gardening, his tractor in hand
He would till and fertilize and work the land
'Til the vegetables showed the fruits of his labors
And there was enough to feed him and his neighbors.

And Senior Citizens was enjoyable as well
With its trips and parties with retired clientele
Even though Dad was not immediately sold
For we remember him saying, "These people are old."

Mom and Dad, your years together have really been good
And while not everything went as you thought it should
Count your blessings, for Mom, as you would say
You have a lot to be thankful for today.

Now fifty years together is a long, long time
But as we've gathered here for food and wine
We hope you're looking forward to more happiness and fun
For remember, after fifty, there's fifty-one.

And each of us whose lives you've touched
Wish to thank you ever so much
For the things you've taught us about the secret to living
That it's loving and sharing, and especially giving.

We wish there were words which we could enlist
To say what we feel at a time like this
But what's in our hearts will have to do
Happy Fiftieth Anniversary and We Love You.

Forty Years and Counting

Joe and Josie, kind of rolls off your tongue
Maybe destined to live and love as one
Joe, I think you know she was the perfect catch
And for forty years, it's been quite a match

How to summarize forty years together
The tears, the laughter, the stormy weather
The trials and tribulations of building a home
And sharing a love few have known

Josie, the busy body, always on the run
Garden to tend, hair to cut – is dinner done?
Queen of the bargain hunters, coupons galore
St. Joseph's table; I really could do more

And where was Joe during those hectic days
Why, out making birdies and taking in some rays
Italian-American, Conewango Member Guest

Couples league, club championship and all the rest
When Joe wasn't golfing and Josie didn't shop
They found time for each other, often as not
It was the look in the eyes, not just luck
That brought along Louise, Dennis and Chuck

And now the grandchildren have come along
The music they make in the heart is like a song
Isabella and Joey, reliving those childhood years
But sending them packing at the first sign of tears

The years have passed so quickly it seems
Josie has slowed down, to a gallop we mean
And Joe is the bionic man, under those jeans
Setting off alarms at the security machines

One other thing we've noticed in recent times
Josie has found golf suits her just fine
She's now making the birdies; bringing home the loot
And showing Joe how to make ten footers to boot

So let's celebrate, raising a glass
To a union of forty years that still lasts
One that's stood the test of time, adversity
To you, Joe and Josie, Happy Anniversary.

Friend

There when you need them, through thick and thin
Soothing when you lose; celebratory when you win
Standing beside you when it's difficult to cope
Through life's darkest days, bringing hope

Happy to spend time together, doing absolutely nothing
Even the smallest occasion turns into something
Secrets shared that will never be heard
Help that comes without even a word

Accepting all our idiosyncrasies and quirks
Rolling up their sleeves when it's time to work
When others talk about you in rumor and lie
They don't participate or even ask why

You have a lot in common; interests you share
In times of trouble, you're in their prayers
Not judgmental or convicting in any way
Much like Jesus modeled for us in his day

They know all your weaknesses and yet you're brothers
Lauding your strengths in front of others
Blind to your limitations, just cannot see
That you're half the person they think you to be

They double your joy; cut your sorrow in half
Spontaneous and raucous when sharing a laugh
They know everything about you, but it's OK
Because nothing you do will drive them away

They're life's treasures, that's for sure
Warming our hearts down to the core
Enriching our lives right to the end
That's why we're blessed to call them 'friend'.

Gone

I awoke one morning and you weren't around
Called your name, but you were not to be found
Asked if you had been seen by any of our friends
And searched for clues for days on end

It took awhile until I realized you'd never return
In the pit of my stomach, something started to churn
Thirty years we'd been together this very year
Yet, in the blink of an eye, you were gone, my dear

As the time passed, I thought of all I'd left unsaid
How petty it seemed now in my hour of dread
Why hadn't I told you you're the lady of my life
And that it was wonderful, you being my wife

That I thought it was great you let me be king
While, behind the scenes, you managed everything
That you were the strength I drew from each day
That I relied on you to show me the way

That I watched in awe how you dealt with others
Shared the joys of the child; the struggles of mothers
Always around with that special touch
The one you can't teach, but means so much.

So why hadn't I told you what was in my heart?
That I needed you every day, right from the start
That you made everything in my life so much better
Why hadn't I written it to you in a love letter?

So if you have something to say to the one you love
Don't let it be just something you're thinking of
Life is unpredictable, stuff happens, and before too long
That special someone who needed those words may be gone.

If the Lord Came to Call

If the Lord came to call and tomorrow never came
I want you to know I'd do it all again
Love you, marry you, care for you, that is
For you're the centerpiece of my happiness

So here's a special gift just for you
Quietly, you'll hear it shout ' I love you'
Thank you for being there through it all
I wanted you to know this if the Lord came to call.

Inner Voice

The years have gone by – in barely a flash
More like a sprint or headlong dash
Than eighteen years on God's endless clock
You're all grown up and leaving the flock!

It's unfortunate neither of us is a wise old sage
To give you the benefit of experience and age
But three things we've learned along the way
May be of some help as you live each day

The first is balance in everything you do
Some nostalgia of old with some glitter of new
Some study hours of intense concentration
Some party time and complete relaxation

Neither worry too much nor be too unconcerned
Know when to be flexible and when stubborn
Pursue your dreams as everyone should
But take time out for a walk in the woods

For many a person has taken the fall
For being too focused or not focused at all
There is certainly merit in never wanting to quit
But it's ok to pause and rest a bit

The second is the joy, in your daily living,
That comes from helping and sharing and giving
For you can never know happiness we truly believe
Unless you willingly give more than receive

The rewarding part of this unselfish style
Is you walk kilometers, but are paid back in miles
Today's minutes and hours you're willing to lend
Are often returned as a lifelong friend

There are two paths from which to choose
You can be a giver or be a Scrooge
But like Ebenezer discovered in his deepest sleep
Whatever you sow, so shall you reap

The third we consider the most important advice
For it has to do with a wonderful device
That always a factor when facing a choice
Unique to you, it's your inner voice

It won't compete for attention in the worldly din
In order to hear it, you have to tune in
But in a quiet moment, alone in your room
It'll seem louder than a sonic boom.

Some call it conscience, some Holy Ghost
In either case, a gift from the Heavenly Host
That, like an alarm in the middle of night
Clearly distinguishes wrong from right

If you will but listen to this voice within
It will free you from the burden of guilt and sin
Knowing the choices you've made are from the soul
And you're a finished work, completely whole

That's about it for this lengthy discourse
Hopefully, these thoughts will always be a source
Of strength and inspiration each and every day
Assuring you never falter or lose your way.

It is Finished: It is Beginning

It is finished, complete the task
Graduate of Mizzou at long last
One day a distant dream to see
The next, a degree in Accountancy.

At times you stumbled more than a bit
But you preserved when others quit
Accepted the challenge, overcame the doubt
Reached deep inside and toughed it out.

A child left home; an adult returned
Much more than book knowledge learned
How to get along, how to deal with stress
How to set a goal and give it your best.

Mom and Dad are so proud of you this day
We pray every success will come your way
And as your responsibilities mount
You may even learn about checking accounts.

It is beginning; a real life that is
New challenges, opportunities, and risks
But if you'll just apply what you've learned in school
There's nothing in this world you can't do.

Jake, the J-Man

Came into the world as Jacob Dennis Mayer
Beautiful eyes, great smile, but no hair
Inquisitive and trying to please everyone
Anyone would be proud to have you as a son

Followed your dad everywhere, tools in hand
We just knew you were going to be a handyman
Then another habit changed our minds
Seems you wanted to pick up trash all the time

Fascinated by heavy equipment, backhoes and such
Would stand for hours watching the men in their trucks
Sometimes the men would lift you up in their rigs
And that little boy was enthralled to be one of the bigs

I think you started driving at the age of two
Four wheelers, golf carts, motorcycles too
We worried about your attention span all the while
Took out grandpa's yard lights with your kamikaze style

In your toddler years, you had the magic touch
Dancing at weddings in your cute little tux
Dazzled us with the footwork of Fred Astaire
We'd all stop what we were doing and stare

Injury-prone, more broken bones than those intact
Many trips to the doctor, that's a fact
Staples in the head, stitches in the chin
Did this boy break his arm again?

Interested in all sports, but not gifted in same
Soccer, basketball, lacrosse just some of your games
But if there were an award for effort all around
You would be the winner, absolutely hands down

Schoolwork did not come easy as it does for some
But you would persist until you got it done
You measure a person's heart by how much they try
And, in that arena, you have reached an all-time high

Jake, you're turning fourteen this year
How did the time fly; the days disappear?
On this occasion we want you to understand
Happy Birthday; we love you J-Man.

Just a Friend

There to listen
Again and again
Not a mother; not a father
Just a friend.

There to support
A hand to lend
Not a brother; not a sister
Just a friend.

There to counsel
Some advice to send
Not a lawyer; not a tax man
Just a friend.

There to critique
Restore discipline
Not a boss; not a boss' boss
Just a friend.

There to laugh
Same old jokes again
Not a buddy; not a neighbor
Just a friend.

There to cry
Hug now and then
Not a son; not a daughter
Just a friend.

There to share
Each little burden
Not a pastor; not a peer
Just a friend.

There to love
Through thick and thin
Not a grandma; not a grandpa
Just a friend.

There to know
The real me within
She's my lover; she's my wife
And yes—my best friend!

On the Way To Fifty

The years are now six and two score
By any measure that's a long, long time
But I'm ready to sign up for more
If you're willing and so inclined

Who knew when we met at the altar
What kind of road we'd traverse
Love would be tested but never falter
A lot of better and very little of worse

It's been quite a journey I have to say
Walking beside you has been a wonderful trip
And I wouldn't want it any other way
Than your hand nestled softly in my grip

What you've taught me in forty-six years
Is a blessing and way beyond measure
You are the best, everything that I revere
And your love is everything that I treasure

I'm not going anywhere until the Lord calls
Because while forty-six seems quite nifty
It's just a stepping stone that we'll recall
Merely one of those milestones on the way to fifty.

Our Little Girl

Well, your first year at Mizzou, an exciting new phase
Only memories remain from your Pioneer days
Blue and White have given way to Black and Gold
My God is our little girl really this old?

Seems only yesterday, that day at DeGraff
When you entered this world, a size and a half
Ah, Brian James, macho man and football bruiser
But wait, it's a girl – a wimp, a loser!

It's taken awhile, but I finally understand
Boys were not part of God's master plan
My life already had baseball and such
What it needed was a sprinkling of the softer touch

For in time I would learn what all of us do
That girls have a way of turning fathers to goo
Your authority is clear, but you're brought to you knees
By those three little words, "Oh, Daddy, please!"

Fond memories we carry of your childhood years,
The giggles, the hugs, the hurt and tears
And we'll never forget the howls and hoots
When you made your appearance in pajamas and boots

Meals were entertaining from that chair on high
Spaghetti in your hair and ear and eye
Hands were preferred, utensils disdained
Nutrition to the bloodstream via the brain

Christmases, then, had a special kind of charm
Whether we stayed at home or went to the farm
For you Christmas was Santa and other magical lies
For us it was the amazement in your big brown eyes

The years have gone by in barely a flash
More like a sprint or headlong dash
Than eighteen years on God's endless clock
You're all grown up and leaving the flock

Lisa, we're so proud of our little girl
Who's stepping out to face the world
We love watching you grow day-by-day
Groping at times, but always finding your way

But as you travel your life's path
Whether it be accounting, psychology, or math
Married or single, children or no
Seize every opportunity and give it a go

We're here to support you in everything you do
We're your parents and we'll always love you
But pardon us for an occasional giggle
We're only remembering when you were little.

Our Spanish Daughter

Across the Pond to America, oh so long ago
Gijon to St. Louis and only 13 years old
Even then confident, you of the Spanish eyes
Little did we know how you'd change our lives

The ride from the airport was quiet and tense
Does what we're doing really make any sense?
We hoped our hospitality would suffice
But a simple game of Uno broke the ice

That first visit was followed by several more
You've seen America from shore to shore
St. Louis, Philadelphia, and Tucson town
We hope you've loved the America you found

You've taught us as well the culture of Spain
Answering some of our questions again and again
And, though you thought it an impossible dream
We've come to see firsthand the Espana scene

We've watched you grow from that clever lass
Happened so quickly, much too fast
You have your own family now, here in Gijon
But there's a place in America that's also your home

You're more than a visitor; more than a friend
You're part of our family, right to the end
We love you just the way a family oughta
Because to us, you see, you're our Spanish daughter.

Short Poems for Family

Mayers' Christmas Gift Delayed

My task was clear; send Mom and Dad's gift
It was a busy day; not much time left
But I sent it on its way; got it off the shelf
Only one problem; I sent it to myself!

Peju Wine Sent for Chandlers Christmas Present

Recalling the what, when and who
Of our Napa Valley run to Peju
Sparing absolutely no cost
To validate "In Vino Veritas"

Love You More

The childhood memories are growing faint
But each year there's a fresh coat of paint
Brighter and more colorful than before
We remember the good times and love you more.

Brighten Your Day

Considered several ideas to brighten your day
But, in the end, there's only one way to say
We love you and as everyone knows
It's best said with a simple rose
After a difficult day, you see
There's always Sophie and me.

Marie Arrives in AZ June 20, 2003

Stargazers for the heart
For the weeks and months apart
Let their aroma ease the pain
And sweeten the times we're together again
Soul mates never again to be alone
I love and missed you, dear
Welcome Home!

Valentine's Day

A rose solitaire
To place in your hair
Or in your teeth clench
Like the mischievous wench
Or drop in a vase
And surround with good taste
Or just hold in your hand
Until you understand
What the world just knows
The love contained in a single rose.
Happy Valentine's Day

The Answered Prayer

Dreams come true; the answered prayer,
Beckoning at our life's door
Behold the child who's standing there,
Offering her love and so much more

A lover she'd be, right from the start –
Hugs and kisses each day.
Unconditionally given, straight from the heart –
More contagious than measles, I'd say

She would be smart, but not flauntingly so,
A mixture of charm and brains
Academic honors would continue to flow,
But cause no character change

A friend she'd be – the forever kind –
Stick with you through thick and thin.
More concerned with those left behind
Than who or what is "in",

Sensitive, yes – but not to a fault
At once, both fragile and strong
Reserves galore in that "inner vault"
To call on when things go wrong

Athletic too – if kamikaze in style,
Pursuing that soccer ball
No wimp here – no, not this child –
Broken toes, bandaged knees and all.

Active in all things – tough, injury prone –
Whether skiing or just riding a bike
With parents away to parts unknown
It's skinned knees, broken thumbs and the like

Of her it'd be said, in honest praise,
From neighbors and teachers, and friends –
"What a nice young lady, Mom and Dad, you raised"
Can any of us expect more in the end?

Dreams come true; the answered prayer
A child lets life begin
We're so glad that you were there
We love you, Deborah Lynn.

Twenty and a Score

The years are now twenty and a score
And there are less days ahead than there were before
But if you grow in the next forty like you did in the first
Ahead of you is the best; behind you the worst.

For while we each have known you only part of this time
We have watched you grow kind of line by line
From the naïve and bubbly lass of Allen Street
To the Sophisticated lady of the St. Louis beat.

One who can handle with seemingly equal dexterity
The checkbook, the menu, the garden and charity
The demands of teenagers and the problems of friends
The moods of the husband – it never ends.

One who is equally at home with executives and paupers
The handicapped, the old, and teeny boppers
One who knows no limits to the spirit of giving
And by her example shows us the secret to living.

One who is at once both fragile and strong
Teaches us discipline and right from wrong
Holds us together in a way only God knows
But self destructs over a solitary rose.

We may not always tell you what we feel inside
Holding it in is a more comfortable ride
But at the big "4-0" you're hitting your heyday
Happy Birthday, dear, you're one super lady.

You Were There

Just an infant, mother, helpless at first
You were my doctor, caregiver, and nurse
Brushing a curl into my wispy hair
Only an infant, but I knew you were there

Then a child, moving at a reckless pace
Cuts and bruises all over the place
A three-foot wrecking ball from hell
But you were there whenever I fell

Then the teenager, the know-it-all
You couldn't tell me much, as I recall
Wasn't much of a listener way back then
But you were there to teach me again and again

Finally, an adult, taking wing from the nest
Life is a journey, a challenge, a test
Through it all, when I stumbled on my own
You were still there to welcome me home

Someday soon my journey will end
Not sure just how; not sure just when
But when I approach Heaven's gate
I know you'll be there, standing in wait.

7
Golf

I have had a lifelong love of the game of golf. It has helped me immensely in business relationships, in building friendships, and in learning some of life's lessons through this wonderful game. One of the golf courses I played many, many times was Bogey Hills Country Club in St. Louis, MO, so that's the basis of the poem, "Ode to Bogey." Golf can be a frustrating game, but many of its challenges are metaphorical challenges for the game of life and that is the essence of the poem, "The Game That Came Down from Heaven." LINKS Players is an organization which believes we can bring others to Christ through the great game of golf.

But Then

The sliced drive that careens into the rough
The hybrid over water, not quite enough
The 8 iron bladed over the green
The bunker shot picked absolutely clean
The frustration sends a message, time to quit
But then, there's the wedge two feet away
And the drive down the middle, crushed more than a bit

There's the shank no one wants to mention this day
The 20 foot chip that's now 40 feet away
The 2 foot putt where you were far too brave
The brand new Titleist in a watery grave
Every part of your being tells you to chuck this game
But then, there's the long downhiller that finds the cup
And the hole out from the sand that salves your pain

There's the round from Hell, double bogeys galore
When drive-by sevens run up your score
When there are no answers despite giving it your best
And you want to pack up your clubs and give it a rest
But then, there's the round just over par
When the putts are dropping and the irons are stiff
When you find your game and know just who you are

So what attracts us to this game as it does
Is it the game we hope for or the game that was
What keeps us coming back when mostly we suffer
Have visions of stardom, but perform like a duffer
I think it's those moments when our shot draws to the pin
And we quietly rejoice in the "But Then."

Golf's Twilight Zone

I could drive the ball long and straight
But I wanted to hit more greens
So I practiced irons until my hands were sore
Soon I was hitting them as never before

I was a good iron player
But I wanted to make more putts
So I practiced putting for hours on end
Until I could make 15 footers again and again

I was a good putter
But I wanted to be able to chip
So I practiced chipping until my back hurt
There wasn't a chip I couldn't convert

I was a good chipper
But I wanted to get up and down from the traps
So I practiced until the bunker was empty of sand
And soon I had that shot pretty well in hand

I was a good bunker player
But I wanted to drive the ball long and straight
And so I went through buckets and buckets one day
Until I could consistently bomb it down the fairway

This game is like a puzzle with a piece always missing
Something always seems like it needs fixing
The day my drives are true, I can't hit greens
And when I can do those two, I can't putt, it seems

But then something happens seemingly out of the blue
It comes at a time when you didn't have a clue
And the frequency is limited, maybe once a year
You're in the zone and everything seems so clear

The driver is driving, the irons are soaring
The putts are dropping; the Tiger is roaring
It all seems so easy it's hard to believe
And it's a wonderful round you're able to weave

So that's why we play this most frustrating game of all
It's not the clubs we use, the latest technique, or the ball
It plays like a concerto piece with just the right tone
You've just crossed over to golf's "twilight zone."

Ode to Bogey

Oh, Bogey! Oh Bogey! How can it be,
Though I've played thee hither and thar
That, after all these swings
Through the trees and things,
I'm still in pursuit of par?

But today's the day; the attitude's right
When my drives will be long and true
My irons will be stiff
And I'll get a lift
From dropping a putt or two

Though the crowd frays my nerves, I take my address
And unleash the initial blow
Can you believe it, man
It cleared the sand
Leaving only a nine iron or so

Be still my head and follow through,
The impact is crisp and clean
From my playing mate,
"The shot is great!"
As it nestles down on the green

My nerves now settled, I stride to two
My confidence is beginning to soar
With solid play
The order of the day
I'm one under through four

Stepping to five, the momentum is strong
I can't recall having such fun
The tempo is smooth
And the swing is grooved
Through six, I'm still negative one

Now I don't know what happened at the seventh hole
The brain just went on the blink
A momentary lapse
Began the collapse
And the ball was in the drink

The recovery attempt was a hacker's delight
About two to three feet off the ground
Bending hard right
An ugly sight
Don't know if it can be found

Three shots were followed quickly by four and five
Golf can be such exquisite pleasure
But my work's not done
There's even more fun
As I three-putt for good measure

There's not much I can say about the rest of the day
It's clear the wheels had come off
Suffice it to say
I began to pray
For mercy from the gods of golf

While the rest of our four played the short grass
I was everywhere, hither and yon
On top of mounds
And out of bounds
And several more in the pond

By the final three holes, I am beside myself,
Totally beaten into submission
"Never again,"
I say to my friends
"Will I embark on such a mission

For today's the day when I end my frustration
I'm leaving this game in the lurch
Fishing and that
Is where it's at
Yeah, salmon and bass and perch

Since I'm resigned to my fate, no more to play
May as well enjoy and relax
Go whither thou will
You white little pill
And may you never come back

That's the attitude with which I approach sixteen
And select a three iron to play
Oh, no! It can't be
That's my ball I see
Lying there three feet away

The putt is uphill and against the grain
But my stroke is firm and true
Well, bless my soul!
It's dead center the hole!
Can you believe it—a two!

The bleeding has stopped! The stride has quickened
The tide has turned for sure
For a well-placed drive and a solid five
Converts seventeen to a four

I confidently attack at the finishing hole,
Keeping my head quite still
The pride is back
It's a mighty whack
I've driven it over the hill

The adrenalin's flowing; I can barely wait
Can't they see this kid's on a roll?
The pin's on the edge
If I can just nip a wedge
It'll cozy on up to the hole

I'm aware of the onlookers as I set up for the shot
My expression is ear-to-ear grin
'Cause the ball's in flight
A beautiful sight
One bounce and it's in!

My celebration is out of control
It's fist bumps /high fives all around
No more sorrow,
Tee time tomorrow?
For I know my game has been found

Oh, Bogey! Oh, Bogey! How can it be
Though I've played hither and thar
That after all these swings
Through the trees and things
I'm still in pursuit of par?

Pledge of Golf

I vow before thee from this day forth
That whenever I set foot upon the course,
Though my ball may fly to parts unknown,
To utter not a single groan.

Nor throw a curse into the air,
Nor walk around in self despair,
But to play each shot as best I can
And return the next day to try again.

I'll do all this, with but one claim
On that rare occasion when I'm on my game
And the ball is landing where I intend
That you'll listen to my replay again and again.

The Game That Came Down From Heaven

We know God created the heavens, the mountains, and the sea
The birds, the plants, the animals, and you and me
But I know when I tell you this you'll probably scoff
Because I also believe God created the game of golf

Bible says, "In the beginning, God created the heavens and earth"
In the Garden of Eden, he transformed Adam from dust to birth
Recognizing a loneliness in Adam that he could not hide
He created Eve, a companion, to always stand by his side

The two were always together, always face to face
And it soon became apparent Adam needed some space
So, seeing Adam viciously beating the ground with sticks
God addressed the problem and hurriedly devised a fix

And so the game of golf was invented way back in ancient when
And man, despite his freedom, would never be the same again
Wandering the earth striking stones toward a hole in the ground
And this all began before the Scots were even around

God sent us golf, not as a game, but as an instructional metaphor
He knew it was a game we'd sometimes love and sometimes abhor
Just as golf comes with its share of loss, struggle and gain
So life is an equal mix of laughter, joy, agony and pain

Each round of golf includes a lesson to be learned
And God selects at least one principle for us to discern
Rejoice in your suffering when the game's not a high
The magnificence of the surrounding tapestry will still please the eye

Obstacles will present themselves in life just as in the game
Overcoming them or not, will your attitude still be the same?
Or will you be so absorbed in yourself and your foolish pride
That you cannot take a win or loss, good or bad, in equal stride

The challenges of life are just sand traps of a different form
The rough just represents the times we wandered off God's norm
Trees are just boundaries that it behooves us to observe
A lucky bounce is the mercy we didn't earn and don't deserve

A double digit score builds character if you persevere
And step up to the next challenge with confidence, not fear
You can play better golf if you can play with a sense of peace
Just as the Lord's forgiveness comes with a sense of release

Staying in the fairway is analogous to a life of righteousness
But stray left or right, your fate is anybody's guess
Taking the good with the bad with no change in mood
Is the Godly way of handling life's vicissitudes

Water is the biggest obstacle of all and like Satan it will take a toll
If we're not focused, our ball will fall into darkness just like our soul
But if we're vigilant and focused on the ultimate prize
Our ball will carry all danger and we'll resist Satan's lies

So can you see now why I credit God for this game of golf
I think it's His game of instruction and correction from far off
Helping us to grow each day, one shot at a time
Until we join Him in Heaven at the end of the line

It just doesn't make sense unless this is the conclusion you reach
Avenues to enlightenment abound and God uses them all to teach
Someday He will have all the answers in that heavenly place
But for now, I believe He invented golf and I rest my case.

The LINKS Player's Creed

You may not have heard of us, but we're LINKS Players
We believe in God and the power of prayer
We believe through golf, we can bring others to the Lord
And that God is pleased when we study His Word

We believe in loving God with all our heart, soul, and mind
And that such love should extend to others in kind
That we must integrate Christ into all we say and do
And that His ancient message is each day refreshing and new

We believe in fellowship with those who share our belief
And that part of our mission is to bring the poor relief
That the Bible is God's Word, His instruction guide
And we know why His Son lived and why He died

We believe through golf we can spread the Good News
That our love of the game is an instrument to be used
To bring others to salvation and Christian livin'
We're not perfect, never will be, but we are forgiven.

The Shot

We complete 18 holes and talk about "the shot"
How far it was, the club we used, and what not
The ball flight—was it a high fade or a low draw?
And did it hit the green with any backspin at all

Yes, the game can be beautiful despite its ups and downs
But we're missing everything if we fail to look around
The mountains are magnificent, pause and take a gaze
The drifting shadows cast a spell in the afternoon haze

Check out what the vibrant flowers have done
Or the emerald fairways, glistening in the sun
Don't miss the azure sky and the wispy or puffy cloud
Pay attention, nature's silently screaming out loud

Note the wildlife--deer, coyote, and quail abound
It may be our golf course, but it's their playground
Witness the feathered masters floating in the air
Red-tailed hawks who catch the thermals there

Say hello to the saguaro cactus as you stroll by
Or the ocotillo blossoms enriching the sky
The roadrunner chattering incessantly at you
The prickly pear showing off its purple hue

So, maybe "the shot" has nothing to do with a ball
Maybe it's really the visual panorama, after all
And we don't need a camera for this sensory high
Because it's all recorded in our mind's eye

Play the game as well as you can, but don't fret
Lasting pleasure doesn't come from the birdies you get
It comes from looking at nature's big board
And giving thanks to its creator, our sovereign Lord.

8
Holidays

Holidays are happy and treasured times of the year, especially since what makes them so is the time spent with family or friends, often family or friends we haven't seen in some time.

Unfortunately, in today's world, we've forgotten in the worst case or overlooked in the best case, why these holidays even exist. These poems are an attempt to bring back a focus as to what holidays like Christmas and Thanksgiving should really mean to us.

America's Blessings

Lord, we look around the world and bear witness
The devil's work causing such distress
Starvation in Somalia; war in the Sudan
Turmoil in the Middle East and Afghanistan

People bathing in open sewers; sleeping on dirt
Nagging hunger; physical and emotional hurt
Families torn apart by war and strife
Struggling to have any semblance of life

Then there's us, Lord, in the USA
Sheltered in warmth; not hungry a day
Hot water and TV's considered a given
Autos and stereos – necessities to livin'

Freedoms of life and liberty a sacred trust
Though we did not earn them; considered a must
Democratic government; religious choice
The right to assemble and raise a voice

Lord, we don't know why you chose this land to bless
Giving us an abundance of all the best
But, on this Thanksgiving, we just want to say
Thank you for all the blessings sent our way

The material things – like houses and clothes
Produce galore – rows upon rows
The intangibles – like friends and health
And, comparatively speaking, our incredible wealth

But, most of all, Lord, it is on this day
That we'd like to thank you in a much different way
Not for material things – by themselves such a waste
But for the awesome power of your unending grace.

Christmas Highlights

Second year in our Arizona home
Amazed at how the time has flown
Finishing the decorating in Southwest taste
And writing checks, but at a slower pace

Neither golf game has really improved
Still searching for that elusive groove
Still chunking, slicing and other flubs
And doing it all with brand new clubs

So many things to do here at SaddleBrooke
Having the time to do them was all it took
Hiking, astronomy, and hot tubbing are all fun
And cocktail hour when the day is done

Some family highlights in 2005
To Wisconsin water park and came out alive
Joe, Lisa, and all the rest
Entered and survived the "Tunnel of Death"

An Arizona visit by Lisa, Debbie and Jake
Kept them busy every moment awake
While the girls spa'd, the boys were messin'
1,000 games of Uno and Jake's golf lesson

Then came the news and a moment of berserk
Jim became a man of leisure, no more work
Years of memories amidst the goodbyes
Jim was retiring the first of July

Still learning how to use our free time best
Keeping the good stuff and leaving out the rest
Some trips in place or to be arranged
North Carolina, Philadelphia and Spain

The holiday spirit here does something lack
Sunny and warm with no coat on your back
But we're muddling through and just wanted to say
To all of you, the very best holiday.

Christmas Reflections

Christmases come and Christmases go
Our memories paint them with a sunset glow
Whenever we ponder these Christmases past
It's with a fondness that forever lasts

There were the baby Christmases; you were so small
No chance you would know Santa at all
But proud parents we were on each of these days
Showing you off in so many ways

Some holidays were trips to the farm
Blankets and PJ's just to stay warm
Cold that would numb you from head to toe
With temperatures that hovered at 20 below

Other years were in Jamestown, feast galore
Gorge ourselves til we could eat no more
Grandparents, children, sisters and brothers
Telling and retelling stories to delight each other

Still the Christmases above all others were those at home
Wherever this vagabond family might roam
Grand Island, St. Louis, or Michigan
The memories are precious to live again

Lisa and Debbie, bakers-in-training gone wild
Giving new meaning to "flour child"
The usual trikes, bikes, dolls and such
And those saucer eyes that said so much

One year we set out to cut our own tree
Having such amusement on this shopping spree
When we lost Mom at the top of the knoll
And turned to see her waist deep in snow

Decorating the tree was a drama in itself
Wouldn't have been pleasing to Santa or elf
But with lights in the wrong place or even worse
The years went by without a divorce

There was the Christmas at Disney World
Our two-foot tree unpacked and unfurled
Christmas Eve was unique I cannot lie
Savoring the taste of Pizza Hut pie

Christmas was outstanding in this magical place
Mickey, Goofy, the rides — not a moment to waste
Fireworks, parades and Christmas luau
We're hungry — what country to dine in now?

And, of course, there was Christmas in Philly
The Charlie Brown tree — now wasn't that silly?
A visitor from Spain in '92
Our laughs with Lucia, more than a few

An Arizona Christmas, in Tucson town
Don't need the coats; don't need the down
Though there is no snow, the spirit's there
A Santa Claus cactus adds to the flair

Now we've come full circle, we're the parents grand
The patter of little feet once again at hand
"Hurry up Santa was here" still sounds the same
Cookies and milk for his visit still part of the game

When we think about what happens each December
There's one special moment we remember
When asked how many gifts Santa had brought
Jake replied "hundreds," without even a thought

Christmases past give way to Christmases in wait
Old memories yield to the ones we create
As our human bytes play and the memories run
It's clear "God has blessed us everyone."

Like an echo the memories rebound
Though now still the original sound.

Christmas, the Acronym

Did you know that Christmas is an acronym?
With each letter standing for something about Him
It all starts and ends, of course, with the **C**hrist
Who came to earth to pay the ultimate price

Then comes **H**onor and glory for the Prince of Peace
This we owe to Him at the very least
Next comes **R**esurrection, death would not win
Christ' appearance restoring life again

Incarnate, taking on flesh this day of his birth
Showing us how we ought to live, here on earth
Sanctification, growing in reliance on the Lord
Marking every day with the study of His Word

We follow on with **T**rust and with it, faith
In return we receive both **M**ercy and grace
Mercy we don't deserve and grace that He sends
Directly to us from our Father and Friend

"**A**" is for **A**lpha and Omega, the beginning and end
Here when it's over; here when it began
"**S**" is for our **S**avior when we needed Him most
Trinity—Father, Son, and Holy Ghost

So Christmas is more than presents under the tree
It's about His presence for you and me
It's a time for us to remember all about Him
And it can be done in a simple acronym.

No Room at the Inn

The Baby Jesus, at birth, had to be laid in a manger
They didn't know who he was; just another stranger
It was not a warm and cozy bed that he slept in
Why—because there was no room for Him at the inn

History has not treated the innkeeper very well
For shunning the Messiah, was he destined for Hell?
Couldn't he have found some kind of accommodation?
For God come to Earth offering hope and salvation?

But aren't we a lot like the innkeeper? No room for God at our inn?
All rooms reserved and occupied much to our chagrin
So that when the Lord knocks on our heart's door
We turn Him away like the innkeeper we abhor

So who or what has filled up all the rooms of our heart?
And can't we clean them out and make a fresh start?
Busyness has lived there for a long, long time
And Greed has positioned himself at the head of the line

Pride has taken up the top floor, the penthouse suite
Living up there with his buddies, Boast and Conceit
Deception has taken up residence just down the hall
Gossip and Slander, permanent residents and that's not all

Selfishness and Control are also welcome guests
Envy, Vanity, and Judgment occupy the rest
So we're really not so much different are we now
From the innkeeper we criticize and disavow?

But if we can purge from our heart these lingering sins
We'll have plenty of room for our Lord to come in
And He won't have to be knocking again and again
We'll have booked a lifetime reservation just for Him.

Reflect on Him

It's Christmas Day, there's magic in the air
The annual gift exchange is about to begin
But lest we forget the gift we all share
Let's take a few moments to reflect on Him

The stockings are hung and filled to the top
And we are about to celebrate with friends and kin
But before the company arrives, let's stop
And take a few moments to reflect on Him

The tree has been trimmed with garland and bow
And the radio is playing our favorite hymn
But we need to keep Christ in Christmas, you know
So take a few moments to reflect on Him

For God's gift to us was His only Son
Who suffered and died to cleanse us from sin
And on the day of his birth, the very least to be done
Is to take a few moments to reflect on Him

So let's not let this opportunity pass
To love and worship Jesus our friend
Let's make him the center of this Christmas
By taking a few moments to reflect on Him

Yes, we all know about Santa at the Pole
His world is magic say the children
But God's world is also magic – to the soul
So let's take a few moments to reflect on Him.

Thanksgiving Blessing

For the stars so bright
For the beauty of the moon's light
For the majestic mountain peaks
For the peace we all seek

For this country, both proud and free
For the Good Samaritan we still see
For the flowers, glorious spread
Gold, violet, satin and red

For the new friends we've made
With whom we've worked and played
For when we first opened Your Word
And decided that indeed, You were Lord
We give thanks.

For our friends and family
Those we think about but seldom see
For those departed, with You this day
For our brave soldiers in harm's way

For our leaders, good and bad
For those sick, weary, or sad
For the helpless victims everywhere, struggling still
For those in bondage against their will

For all of these on this day
We raise them up, Lord, and pray.
Amen.

That Ordinary You

The night was ordinary in every way
The dark overcame the light in the usual way
Maybe there was a gust of wind somewhere
Or maybe there was a hint of chill in the air

Maybe it was a beautiful night in December
But it wasn't one likely you'd remember
Not one of surprise to keep you awake
No fiery red sunset over a peaceful lake

The sheep were on the hillside bedded down
Most eyes closed, not making a sound
Just lumps in the night, silhouettes
Loved as a master would love his pets

The shepherds were there, destitute and poor
None of their clothes bought at a department store
They were a simple and nameless lot
Knowledgeable and worldly they were not

Ordinary night, ordinary shepherds, ordinary sheep
Nothing you'd write in your journal to keep
Were it not for the Lord, this night would pass
Without anything to remember or anything to last

But the Lord deals everyday with the ordinary
And his hand quickly transforms it to extraordinary
The common becomes uncommon for a reason
And 2000 years later we celebrate the season

Suddenly, the sky explodes; shepherds on their feet
Sheep, once content, are a chorus of bleat
The night would be ordinary no more
His Son had come to earth as prophesied before

That's God's workplace—simple, ordinary, and weak
The ones who need him most are the ones He seeks
All of our limitations, our imperfections, and sins
That's where the power of the Lord begins

So, if you'll just bring Him your ordinary stuff
His awesome strength and love are more than enough
To transform your life, make it exciting and new
And you won't recognize that ordinary you.

The Greatest Gift Exchange of All

There's a special kind of excitement in the air
No other time of the year involves as much fanfare
We move from store to store and it gives us a lift
When, for that dear friend, we find just the right gift

There's heartfelt anticipation of the day to come
When our divisions are set aside and we are one
Christmas day arrives and everything is arranged
Let the joy begin—it's the great gift exchange

But how many of us consider how this all got its start?
The one time we share with our loved ones what's in our heart
When our feelings tell us what all along we believed
That it's infinitely better to give than it is to receive

Shall we go back to the beginning for the solution?
When God sent his Son for complete resolution
Of the rift that had developed between Him and man
We had proven we were hopeless, but God had a plan

God created us, He loved us, and He gave us His Son
That was some gift all wrapped up in The One
And all we had to do was just accept the Gift with a yes
And follow His lead with unwavering faithfulness

That was the first gift exchange that set the trend
Of giving to each other, neighbor and friend
Everlasting life with God if you just accept the call
And participate in the Greatest Gift Exchange of all.

The Ultimate Gift

Twas the night before Christmas; all the hoopla turned down
It was quiet as a mouse all over town
Shopping done, stockings hung, end of the rush
In every corner of the house, a welcome hush

We were all tucked away, snug in our beds
Christmas morning visions danced in our heads
Suddenly, there appeared a penetrating light
So overwhelming, it extinguished the night

I leapt out of bed, in a complete dither
Not knowing where to run, yon or hither
Just as my choice was about to be made
There came this voice, "don't be afraid"

The apparition was shimmering and oh so bright
Shielding my eyes, I shivered in fright
My heart was racing, my blood pressure high
Then came the voice, "It is I"

"It is I, the first and the last
Not the ghost of Christmas future or Christmas past
I who knew you before you were born
Who has been with you since the curtain was torn"

It's okay, the Santa Claus myth
But I'm here to offer you the ultimate gift
The one for which He suffered at Calvary
Paying the price of our sins for all eternity"

As He spoke, a quiet peace settled on my soul
I accepted His gracious gift and reborn role
There were changes coming in my behavior
And I would teach my children of our Lord and Savior

I awoke to pitter patter and a child's scream
But this experience was more than just a dream
Santa Claus would continue to visit our place
But we'd also make room for His amazing grace

Church would no longer be just an obligation
There'd be time for prayer and celebration
I had accepted the Holy Spirit's call
It truly would be a Merry Christmas for all.

9
On Getting Old

They say only two things in life are certain—death and taxes. I think there is another—while we're on earth, we're all getting older. We obviously can't turn back the clock, but we can laugh at ourselves and look for new outlets to live in a meaningful way.

A New Passion

I wear glasses, but I can't see
In the bathroom I'm slow to pee
The hair that used to grow on my head
Now grows in my nose and ears instead

Belly fat resides where I used to be thin
It's complemented by the fat on my double chin
The skin once tight now flabby and loose
When I breathe it's like the call of the moose

The droopy eyelids tell of years passed
Bags under the eyes are expanding fast
Veins are popping out everywhere I look
And liver spots just complete the look

My gait is slower and painful to watch
Those following ask me to pick it up a notch
My short-term memory is shot to hell
But 40 years ago is clear as a bell

Sitting down cannot be done without a groan
And getting back up is arduous alone
A common question starts with "what"
Someone tells you to turn the volume up

So what shall we do in these fading years
When we're falling apart and the last act nears?
Will we find a new gig or just fold up our tent?
Will we find some happiness or just discontent?

There's no doubt our physical self is declining
But there's no reason to be melancholy or wining
The spirit that drives us is alive and well
And it behooves to tap into that and break the spell

May I suggest taking the focus off yourself
And focus on others who need your help
And when you do, something vibrant will begin
A feeling of renewal, of being younger again

It's passion that drives our spirit to new heights
And hides the darkness of our autumn nights
Look around; find something wonderful and new
And you'll discover that lost energy if you do

Our bodies may be failing, that's for sure
And physically, we're not the person we were before
But our spirit can still be filled with love and compassion
And all we have to do is find a new passion.

The Older I Get

Each year my SAT scores inch a little higher
My life resonates with passion and fire
My athletic accomplishments reach a higher bar
A journeyman player transforms to a star

In academia, my name frequents the honor roll
Even though my grades were just average or so
An eloquent delivery when it was my turn to speak
Not the stammering bore who'd put you to sleep

In social circles, always running with the hip, in-crowd
Even though the girls I knew were never wowed
That sluggish old sedan becomes the sporty, sleek kind
At least that's how it all plays out in my mind

Even though I never became the executive- in- charge
I still found a way to keep living large
Recalling each accolade as it came my way
And the legend grows with each passing day

Time has colored the life that I remember now
In the retelling, the facts just blur somehow
I don't know why that is but I think it's because
The older I get, the better I was.

10
Travel

My wife and I have been blessed with the financial resources to travel to some amazing places in the United States and the world—Alaska, Israel, Ireland, Mexico, Bermuda, the Mediterranean, and most of our national parks. Each of those places left a lasting impression on us and made us realize first of all what a beautiful country we live in, and secondly that we have a lot more in common with other people in the world than we have differences. The more we understand other cultures, it seems to me, the less likely we are to be at war with each other.

Arctic Accolades

Philadelphia to Toronto to Vancouver
Through security, customs, check-in maneuver
A short ride cross town and we're witness
To the magnificent Ocean Princess

Give her the once over bow to stern, starboard to port
Tuscan Restaurant, Atrium Lounge, and Horizon Court
Swimming pools, hot tubs, workout room and more
Then chug up the stairs to 11, the Aloha Floor

To call our room a closet is to expand its scope
But the balcony out the back makes it easy to cope
Mooring lines untied, we push off land
Anniversary to celebrate in Ketchikan

A day at sea—time to recoup and meet new friends
A little R & R and we're in Ketchikan
Dock right there in the middle of town
Look for things to do and shop around

Several anniversary activities would have held no risk
Kayaking not one of them—we, of course, choose this
Though we look like dancing bears in tutu skirts
We emerge—marriage still intact and feelings unhurt

That night in the Tuscan with elegance we dine
35 years to celebrate with a touch of wine
Just the two of us, fixed on each other's eyes
A special evening with anniversary surprise

In dreamland, the Princess slips quietly north
Arrive the next morning in Juneau, capital port
Head for the wharf, a floatplane to hail
Climb aboard with the rest of the "killer whales"

Taku Lodge our destination as we ride water and air
Fjords, glaciers, and eagles the common fare
Nothing could top the hospitality at this retreat
Except the bears who made our trip complete

Back in town and parched by late afternoon
We brush through the doors of the Red Dog Saloon
A throwback entertainer as the Gold Rush would befit
The "boat people" are captivated by his music and wit

So long, Juneau—we're on our way
Looking for gold in ole Skagway
New friends we meet at the wine-tasting swill
Patsy and Perry, Karen and Bill.

In Skagway, the adventures just continue on
We embark on the Alaskan quadrathalon
Catamaran, bus ride, hike and canoe
Paddling to Davidson Glacier is really cool

In the afternoon, it's the streetcar tour
Molly, our host, knows the town that's for sure
Tell the story of Soapy Smith with gusto she could
Officially inducted into the Arctic Brotherhood

We push further north to Glacier Bay
Watch the sea otters and harbor seals at play
To awesome Margerie Glacier we cruise
And marvel at the ice that calves on queue

College Fjords next up on the cruise
Glaciers all named for Ivy League schools
Glacier terminology by now we've mastered
As we gaze upon Holyoke, Harvard, and Vassar

The cruise is complete at Seward's Folly
Anticipating "The Great One", a.k.a. Denali
But first a stop for lunch in Anchorage town
Some reindeer sausage and more shopping around

On to the Princess Lodge, hoping to be blessed
With a view of Denali's magnificent crest
Hidden from the world most of the time
Today's our day; the weather's just fine

To the back deck we're inevitably lured
Fully awestruck at her snowy grandeur
Hardly seems real, more like a cloud
We feast in reverence; even God must be proud

Dinner on the deck is absolutely right
Hard to be critical with such a splendid sight
Of the mountain's majesty we do regale
And enjoy a glass or two of Moose's Tooth ale

On to Denali, arrive before dark
Next day bus ride to the National Park
One so wild, untouched, and vast
Rival in size to the state of Mass

As we traverse the tundra—valley and ridge
And peer at caribou, moose, and grizz
Follow wolf and lynx stalking their prey
We become tree huggers, at least for a day

One last adventure – raft Nenanee River water white
In dry suit garb and vest, we're quite the sight
Class III waves crash over bow and side
Twelve miles through the canyon—what a ride

Our trip is ended; we have to depart
A piece of Alaska always in our heart
We'll not forget this last frontier
Or how we celebrated 35 years.

He's Alive

We came from different parts, this disciple band
A common goal in mind—visit the Holy Land
To walk where Jesus walked so long ago
To strengthen our faith and renew our soul

First stop, Caesarea, where Cornelius made news
God's family would not be exclusive to the Jews
The Gentiles would be grafted onto the vine
And have the opportunity for salvation for all time

On to Nazareth where they rejected their own
How could this carpenter boy be connected to the throne?
He even had the gall to heal the Gentiles and not the Jews
Because they just couldn't accept the Good News

Next up, Mount of Beatitudes, above the sea
Heard the secret to happiness is not fueled by greed
Blessed means God's joy and it doesn't start
With merit badges and pride, but flows from the heart

A highlight of the trip for sure, baptismal site
Not John, but Max who performed the rite
Is Jesus the son of God the question at hand
Waded into the Jordan and left a new man

Then it's on to Jerusalem, God's Holy Place
So much history here, times of judgment and grace
From the Temple steps we hear Jesus is ruler of all
And all we have to do is answer the call

We trace the Lord's path from the Olive Mount
Imagining His followers too numerous to count
Laying their cloaks and branches at His feet
Not a horse, but a donkey for the Prince of Peace

We recall Jesus' wrath at the money changers in the Temple
And yet still today, merchants set the same example
We visit the Upper Room and the Garden of Gethsemane
Jesus obeying God's plan to save you and me

Via Dolorosa— in English, the way of agony
Aptly describing how Christ suffered for humanity
Carrying that ugly cross up and up to the top of the hill
And nailing our sins to it per His Fathers' will

The climax of the trip, a visit to the Garden Tomb
Jesus' body would not be confined to this earthen room
The massive rock would move and roll away
And He'd be spiritually and physically alive another day

We had all taken communion hundreds of times
With rituals and services in churches of all kinds
But with the birds chirping in this garden there
And not a dry eye, nothing will ever compare

We were all drawn to this trip in one way or another
This assemblage of Christians, this band of brothers
Death could not hold our Lord in this earthly prison
We know He's alive; we know He's risen

Icicle River

My gaze is transfixed in my reverie
The magnificent Icicle River streams by me
Its waters racing to I know not where
Awesome, though, in how it gets there

It churns and dips and dives in its downward run
Its roar a splendid symphony never quite done
Did it get its name from its wintry cold
Or was it the beauty the icicle holds?

One thing I know as I watch it impress
This couldn't have happened by chance I confess
No – God's hand is apparent in all I see
You cannot witness this and not believe.

Irish Memories

Our backgrounds varied; we came from different parts
Golf, the common passion, embedded in our hearts
Brought us together to share a few days
To play a few rounds and a Guinness or two raise

We've learned much about Ireland and made new friends
But our time in this tranquil setting is nearing an end
For tomorrow we'll return to homes here and there
And all we'll have left is the memories we've shared

And what memories they are too, the golf thirst to quench
Ballybunion, Waterville, Tralee, and Lahinch
Real Irish golf at Waterville and Bally B
But also more sunshine than any could believe

We chased that little pill up and over the mounds
Along the ocean, the beach, and out of bounds
Hacked through the heather and slashed through the gorse
Slicing, hooking, ballooning, and worse

But, at the end of the day, there was always a pub
Toss down a Guinness and sample the grub
From corned beef and cabbage to real Irish stew
And maybe end the day with a "triscuit" or two

How could we ever forget Johnny, the perfect host
As the years pass, it's he we'll remember the most
Giving us the historical perspective on all that we see
And, along the way, attending to our every need

There will also be the personal memories, you know
From John Case making it four years in a row
To her majesty, the Queen, and her Princess Court
To the non-golfers making shopping a whole new sport

From Terry and Steve, the "Nightline Team"
Was it at "Murphy's" or "Scruffy's" they were last seen?
To Lee's club toss, in the rain and the gale
To Joe Paul's repertoire of Texas tales

When we hit a poor shot, we mean no malice
If you hear us yell, "where the ____ is Alice?"
There's Vince still trying to collect on his bet at Tralee
And Carol with her "almost eagle" at Bally B

Marv and Kathy's anniversary fete was just fine
And don't forget Esther's 40 on the back nine
We can still hear the ribbing, jeering and scoff
When the Tayburns had the nerve to take a day off

From beginning to end, a vacation of the highest rate
And Johnny was never thirty minutes late
To Jerry, Johnny and Patty this trip's been one of a kind
And especially to Johnny, we've had a "divil" of a time.

Israel in a Minute

Oh my, it's green
Galilee, so serene
Jerusalem, high on a hill
Focus of God's plan—still
The original Men in Black
Jesus rose; that's a fact
Sermons in all the right places
Joy on so many faces
Jericho town
How did those walls all come down?
Ruins on top of ruins—don't Tel
Armageddon—heaven vs. hell
The Upper Room
The Garden Tomb
Masada, the fortress above
Laugh, learn, leave, and love
The shepherd leading his flock
The Bedouins, stepping back in the clock
Bag a banana along the way
Fish hatcheries almost every day
The cross up to Calvary
The scrolls from the Dead Sea
Mount of Beatitudes and that's not all
The Temple steps and the Western Wall
Eleven buses to cart us around
Take the steps up; take the steps down
To the Jordan; rededicate
Christ returning through the Golden Gate
And the last thing to include in our file
When leaving the smiley, be sure to smile.

Old Blue Eyes and Dr. No

City of Angels, cruise rendezvous point
Mexican Riviera, please don't disappoint
This trip a surrogate for one to St. Lou
Quality time with son-in-law and Lisa Lou

Days at sea, mostly happiness and bliss
Fun and sun aboard the Sapphire Princess
No chance of going ashore, what shall we do?
Maybe stop by for a martini or two

Crooner's Lounge, highlight of the cruise
Drink too sophisticated to call it booze
Even Sinatra and Bond would love this show
Mixing up Old Blue Eyes and Dr. No

Sam's quite the smoozer, we can attest
Does the martini dance for all of his guests
Each day's fantastic, wherever we go
Because it ends with Old Blue Eyes and Dr. No

Running the zip lines and yachting are quite the blast
Which restaurant did we eat at last?
Wine tasting, swimming pool, a bucket or so
Dinner time for Mr. James and Mr. Joe

But whenever we reminisce about this cruise
Taking a moment to reflect and muse
We'll reach for the shakers and give them a go
And recall Old Blue Eyes and Dr. No.

Remembering Bermuda

Tripping aboard the Celebrity Cruise
New York skyline, magnificent views
JP's jaw dropping, a sight to see
At the arrival of Jim and Marie

Time spent at the Martini Bar
Jim and Karen took it just a bit too far
Joe C. in the full mode of panic
Seems they checked him out mid Atlantic

Wonderful hosts for dinner, don't you know
Egbert, Andre, and Julio
Every now and then a questioning cry
Where, oh where, is the wine guy?

Joe C., always the extra service mile to go
Lowering a bottle of scotch to the balcony below
Rick and Jim, with medicine in the gut
Posing for pictures, hand on butt

Josie wasn't to be satisfied any time soon
Seems she just can find the right spoon
Rick's entrance, Bermudasized head to toe
Great look; not for dinner though

Chandlers and Tayburns not to be seen
Bet they took the high road to Q-Sine
Savoring the gastronomic el tour
A true dining event to be sure

Mopeds here, there, and everywhere
Rent one to ride if you dare
Beaches, best in the world
Colored by nature, pink and pearl

Not the kind of roads you'd call wide
Better keep your hands and arms inside
Lest they be clipped off in the ongoing rush
By overhanging tree or a passing bus

We had heard it all before
'Bout the Triangle; all the lore
But just so you have all the facts
We ran right through it without a scratch

Quite a cruise, all in all
As we return to our port of call
It's safe to say over the ocean miles
That we had a blast in the Bermuda Isles.

Standing on the Galilee

Standing on the shore of the Galilee
Just the Lord, my Savior, and me
Be still and know that I am God
A message as I walk where Jesus trod

His story started on this very shore
A touch of history, yes, but so much more
His voice rings softly and clear
There are no distractions for my ear

It's peaceful, quiet, a world asleep
And I pray to Him my soul to keep
To protect me from the gates of Hell
To renew my faith here in Israel

I know not what's ahead or even how far
But I know He's the potter; I'm just the jar
I'm willing to be remade, to follow His Way
I believe it all starts for me this day

I want to laugh; I want to learn
Knowing it's to Him I can always turn
To love Him and others; throw away my pride
Nothing is impossible with the Lord by my side.

About the Author

Jim Tayburn grew up on a dairy farm in central New York State, and while he still treasures the values that such a life instills, he knew he wanted something more. He left for the University of Buffalo and never looked back. His 37 year sales and marketing career with Occidental Petroleum took Jim and his wife, Marie, to Michigan, St. Louis, and Philadelphia, as well as Buffalo. They have witnessed firsthand the cultural and geographical landscape of living in the United States and feel blessed to have done so.

Jim and Marie retired to Tucson, Arizona in 2005 and fell in love with the beauty and amazing diversity of life in the Sonoran Desert. They have two daughters and three grandchildren who live in the East. Jim says that if there is one downside to living out West, that is it.

His favorite poets are Robert Frost and Rudyard Kipling, because their poems *The Road Not Taken* and *If* are classics, each with a message that is simple and profound at the same time.

www.ingramcontent.com/pod-product-compliance
Lightning Source LLC
Chambersburg PA
CBHW022359040426
42450CB00005B/256